FISHERS OF MEN

GERALD MCDANIEL

WESTBOW
PRESS®
A DIVISION OF THOMAS NELSON
& ZONDERVAN

WestBow Press books may be ordered through booksellers or by contacting:

WestBow Press
A Division of Thomas Nelson & Zondervan
1663 Liberty Drive
Bloomington, IN 47403
www.westbowpress.com
844-714-3454

Scripture taken from the King James Version of the Bible.

ISBN: 978-1-6642-3137-5 (sc)
ISBN: 978-1-6642-3138-2 (e)

Print information available on the last page.

WestBow Press rev. date: 4/30/2021

A Personal Letter to my Grandchildren

I would like to share, first of all, a partial personal testimony out of my own life. Many years ago, as a small young boy I was extremely shy and very much an introvert. I would do most anything to avoid standing up in front of people and speaking especially in front of a school class. Even in sports on the basketball court the intimidation of the crowd no matter how large or small would greatly hinder me from playing basketball as well as I was able.

I had a dear grandmother who was a precious Christian lady. When she would come to stay with our family from time to time, she would always call me her little preacher boy. I hated it because even though I was lost at the time I knew that it would mean getting up in front of people. Needless to say, I regretted it every time grandmother came around.

At the age of 20 years old I trusted Christ as my personal Savior. At the age of 21 years old, strange as it may seem, God called me to preach. My grandmother was right.

Having said this I am convinced just like grandmother was that I will have a grandchild whether born or adopted, girl or boy that God will call to take the books that I have written and learn them and be able to understand them and teach from them and use them in their ministry that God has for them.

Be advised, you will run into many that do not agree with the teachings in these books. You will probably have family that will not agree with the teachings in these books. Either way as a little girl in writing or teaching ladies or as a little boy in writing or teaching and preaching, I am convinced God will raise up one of my grandchildren to a ministry that these books will be greatly used.

Please understand at the time of this writing, there have been 4 books published and 2 written yet to be published with more to come. At this time, you may not even be born yet or adopted yet. Even though all my grandchildren are welcome to these books and will have access to these books, I am convinced as much as I am alive that God will raise up one of you with a special ministry directly related to these books.

If I live long enough, I will be able to witness this taking place, firsthand. My grandmother died before she was able to hear me preach. Please be aware that I am not writing these books as a hobby neither are they written to make money. It is a God called ministry. There will be many more books written and all my grandchildren will have access to them if that is their desire. I want to reassure you of course that I love all my grandchildren.

There will be one with a special calling. May God bless you little one and I am praying for you now even if you have not been born or adopted yet. Granddaddy loves you very much and is excited about what God will do in your life.

This letter will be published with the future books to make sure you get a copy of this letter.

Contents

1

The Plan of Salvation

Let's go through **4 H's. Honesty, Humility, Helpless, and Hope**

H   #1)   *You must be **HONEST** enough to admit you have sinned and broken God's commands. Understand in doing so this puts you in very great danger!*

Romans 3:10 "there is none righteous, no not one."

Romans 3:23 "…all have sinned…"

I John 1:8 "if we say that we have no sin, we deceive ourselves, and the truth is not in us."

H   #2)   *You must be **HUMBLE** enough to admit you deserve Hell when you die.*

One sin disqualifies us from Heaven, and we have all sinned more than once.

1

Romans 6:23 "For the wages of sin [is] death"

Revelation 21:8 "But the fearful, and unbelieving, and the abominable, and murderers, and whoremongers, and sorcerers, and idolaters, and all liars, shall have their part in the lake which burneth with fire and brimstone: which is the second death."

H   #3)   *You must understand you are **HELPLESS** when it comes to you saving yourself from going to Hell when you die. There is nothing you can do to pay for your own sin.*

Ephesians 2:8-9 For by grace are ye saved through faith; and that not of yourselves: it is the gift of God: not of works, lest any man should boast.

Titus 3:5 Not by works of righteousness which we have done, but according to his mercy he saved us, by the washing of regeneration, and renewing of the Holy Ghost;

Galatians 2:16 Knowing that a man is not justified by the works of the law, but by the faith of Jesus Christ, even we have believed in Jesus Christ, that we might be justified by the faith of Christ, and not by the works of the law: for by the works of the law shall no flesh be justified.

Understand when I say HELPLESS it means you cannot surrender your life to Christ for salvation. You have no life to surrender. You are dead in trespasses and sins. You cannot yet make Jesus the Lord of your life because you have no life.

Jesus will not be Lord of your life until He is Savior of your soul. You cannot turn from your sins because you are dead in your sins. You must see yourself HELPLESS at the Mercy of God. Now you are ready for H # 4.

H   #4) *You are helpless but not hopeless. Your* **HOPE** *must be in Jesus, God's Son and what he has done for you on the cross when He died there. Jesus is the only one that paid for your sins when he died on the cross. He was buried and arose again. You must ask Jesus to be your personal Savior and ask Jesus to save you from Hell. If you are depending on church membership to save you, that means you are not depending on Jesus to save you. If you are depending on the good deeds you do to save you, that means you are not depending on Jesus to save you. If you are depending on baptism to save you, that means you are not depending on Jesus to save you. It must be Jesus and what Jesus did for you on the cross that you are depending on to save you. Nothing else can go with this. Jesus is the only one who paid for your sins on the cross so Jesus is the only one who can save you.*

Romans 5:8 But God commendeth his love toward us, in that, while we were yet sinners, Christ died for us.

I Peter 3:18 For Christ also hath once suffered for sins, the just for the unjust, that he might bring us to God, being put to death in the flesh but quickened by the Spirit.

Hebrews 10:12 But this man (JESUS) after he hath offered one sacrifice for sins for ever, sat down on the right hand of God.

John 14:6 Jesus saith unto him, I am the way, the truth, and the life: no man cometh unto the Father, but by me.

Acts 4:12 Neither is there salvation in any other: for there is none other name under heaven given among men, whereby we must be saved.

John 3:16 For God so loved the world, that he gave his only begotten Son, that whosoever believeth in him should not perish, but have everlasting life.

Ask Jesus to save you before it is too late:

Romans 10:13 For whosoever shall call upon the name of the Lord shall be saved.

2

Opening Comments

One of the most exciting things a believer can learn to do is to yield to God for God to make him or her a **Fisher of Men**. For over 40 years I have personally gone door to door soulwinning and witnessing in all kinds of neighborhoods in many towns, cities, and states. I have never been bored. I have been cursed at, dog bit, threatened, threatened with a gun, blessed out, blessed, and thanked but never bored. The personal experiences and episodes of each visit are diverse and typically quite thrilling. When you approach the front door of a home that you have never been to before you can never know what is going to happen until that door opens. You would think after so many years that you have seen it all, but trust me, you may have seen a lot, but you will never see it all.

To be a **Fisher of Men** is both an honor and it will give you a great since of fulfillment and gratification like nothing else will. You will be fulfilling the real purpose that God has for you that very few believers will fulfill. Notice the following passages about this wonderful work of becoming a **Fisher of Men**.

Matt 4:19 And he saith unto them, Follow me, and I will make you **fishers of men**.

Mark 1:17 And Jesus said unto them, Come ye after me, and I will make you to become **fishers of men.**

Comparing this to the military, in the Army you would be a Ranger or a Green Beret. In the Navy you would be a Seal. In the Christian world you would be a "Fisher of Men." As a fisher of men, you are a Soldier of Christ. Notice the following passage.

2Tim 2:3 Thou therefore **endure hardness, as a good soldier of Jesus Christ**. **2Tim 2:4** No man that warreth entangleth himself with the affairs of *this* life; that he may please him who hath **chosen him to be a soldier**.

You will notice that in order to become a fisher of men, you will have to follow Christ. Before we can follow Christ, we must be sure that we first have trusted Christ as our own personal Savior. You must not only have the assurance of your salvation, you must also have the joy of your salvation. You will not be able to help give others assurance and joy of their salvation if you do not have it yourself. Please study Chapter one of this book and make sure that you are saved. A bogged down truck cannot pull out a bogged down truck. Notice the order that Christ gives. He says first to follow Him or to come after Him. Do not seek to be a fisher of men as a fad. A believer is not to approach this upon a whim. This is not something you pick up and do because everyone else is doing it. Trust me, very few believers are doing this and believe it or not, very few preachers are doing this. It is a very miserable task to get in the pulpit on Sunday when you have not gone soulwinning on the Saturday before. To follow Christ as a believer is to change your life and lifestyle and do what Jesus would have you do in every detail of your life to the best of your ability. The motive is clear on why you should. Notice the next passage.

John 14:15 <u>If ye love me, keep my commandments.</u>

Your motive for following Christ is your love for Christ. Paul said it this way.

2Cor 5:14 For <u>the love of Christ constraineth us</u>;

When you decide to follow Christ, you will realize the Bible, which is God's Word, lays out the steps God wants you to take in your life. Notice the next passages.

Ps 37:23 <u>The steps of a *good* man are ordered by the LORD</u>: and he delighteth in his way.

Ps 119:133 <u>Order my steps in thy word</u>: and let not any iniquity have dominion over me.

Matt 4:4 But he answered and said, It is written**, Man shall not live by bread alone, but by every word that proceedeth out of the mouth of God.**

Rom 12:1 I beseech you therefore, brethren, by the mercies of God, that ye **present your bodies a living sacrifice, holy, acceptable unto God,** *which is* your reasonable service. **Rom 12:2** And **be not conformed to this world: but be ye transformed by the renewing of your mind, that ye may prove what *is* that good, and acceptable, and perfect, will of God**.

As the believer learns to follow Christ more and more, Jesus makes an interesting statement. Jesus said, "I will make you" or "I will make you to become fishers of men."

In spite of a world filled with unbelievers, the percentage of believers who are fishers of men is extremely small. Notice the following passages.

Matt 9:37 Then saith he unto his disciples, **The harvest truly *is* plenteous, but the labourers *are* few;**

Luke 10:2 Therefore said he unto them, **The harvest truly *is* great, but the labourers *are* few**: pray ye therefore the Lord of the harvest, that he would send forth labourers into his harvest.

So, as you read this book, this author would like to impart upon each reader the burden to help reach this world for Christ one soul at a time. You will be rare, and you will meet very few that are fishers of men, but you will be blessed. I am not referring to you becoming a world traveler. I am more concerned about you reaching your own neighborhood and community and town. Notice the following passages.

Acts 20:20 *And* how I kept back nothing that was profitable *unto you*, but have shewed you, and **have taught you publickly, and from house to house**,

Luke 14:23 And the lord said unto the servant, **Go out into the highways and hedges, and compel *them* to come in**, that my house may be filled.

Acts 2:46 And they, continuing daily with one accord in the temple, and **breaking bread from house to house**, did eat their meat with gladness and singleness of heart,

One of the many benefits of being a fisher of men is the speed that God will teach the witnessing believer the Bible. Notice the following passage.

Prov 11:30 The fruit of the righteous *is* a tree of life; and **he that winneth souls *is* wise.**

God will train you and teach you many things from the Bible in order to help you witness to others and answer their questions and help others to get saved and to get grounded after salvation.

God thinks so highly of each "Fisher of Men" that when they get to heaven God gives a special reward just for them. Notice the following passage.

1Thess 2:19 For what *is* our hope, or joy, or **crown of rejoicing**? *Are* not even ye in the presence of our Lord Jesus Christ at his coming? **1Thess 2:20** For ye are our glory and joy.

Meeting the individuals that we have led to Christ up in heaven some day and receiving the Crown of Rejoicing will be a very rewarding experience.

Please study this book carefully and prayerfully and you will learn more about what it means to become a **Fisher of Men**.

3

The Command from God to Go

In this chapter this author would like to share with the reader a few passages in the Bible where God commands every believer to witness. This command is neglected by many believers.

The Great Commission

Matt 28:19 <u>Go ye therefore, and teach all nations</u>, baptizing them in the name of the Father, and of the Son, and of the Holy Ghost: **28:20 <u>Teaching them to observe all things whatsoever I have commanded you</u>**: and, lo, I am with you alway, *even* unto the end of the world. Amen.

It is true that this great commission was first given by God to the apostles. However, in verse **20** God tells the apostles to teach other believers all things God commanded them. One of those things God commanded them is to go and teach all nations. So, each believer should take this commandment personally for themselves.

Mark 16:15 And he said unto them, <u>**Go ye into all the world, and preach the gospel to every creature.**</u>

1Pet 3:15 <u>**But sanctify the Lord God in your hearts: and *be* ready always to *give* an answer to every man that asketh you a reason of the hope that is in you with meekness and fear**</u>:

Acts 1:8 But <u>**ye shall receive power, after that the Holy Ghost is come upon you: and ye shall be witnesses**</u> unto me both in <u>**Jerusalem**</u>, and in <u>**all Judaea**</u>, and in <u>**Samaria**</u>, and unto the <u>**uttermost part of the earth**</u>.

Allow me from the passage above to share with you a personal application from the four parts of the world and to make them apply to the four parts of each believer's world.

I. **Jerusalem: The Domestic:**
    The domestic in your world and in your neighborhood would be the home grown. These are people that were born in the immediate area and are well set in their ways and their beliefs whether they are right or wrong. You would probably hear from them statements like, "This is the way we have always done it" or "This is the way we have always believed" with many of them not even being aware of what the Bible teaches. Many of them will think they are saved because their mom and dad were saved.

II. Judaea: The Devout:

The devout in your world are those that you will meet that are very religious and some of them are lost and some are saved. The lost are typically lost in their own religion. These typically are depending on their works and deeds that they do to get them to heaven and typically would mock real salvation and eternal security. They typically believe that you can lose your salvation.

III. Samaria: The Disdained:

The disdained in your world are those that are the misfits of that overall society. They would not fit in anywhere. They may be of a different race or financially unstable or poor or from another state or country. They are socially unacceptable by the general population, but these typically are the ripest in the harvest field and the first that are wanting to hear the gospel and show very little resistance when it comes to receiving the gospel.

IV. Uttermost Part of the Earth: The Distant:

The distant in your world are those that would be classified as the hermits of your neighborhood and society. They are very withdrawn from public and are the ones most unlikely to go to church on their own. They have isolated themselves from the rest of the neighborhoods and they typically keep to themselves.

As a fisher of men, you must be prepared to reach them all. May God give you the wisdom and heart to be concerned with all that are in your world. Everyone in your local world around you fits into one of these four categories. God loves them all so you must do what you can be the grace of God to reach them all.

1Pet 3:15 But sanctify the Lord God in your hearts: and ***be* ready always to *give* an answer to every man** that asketh you a reason of the hope that is in you with meekness and fear:

Matt 22:9 <u>Go ye therefore into the highways</u>, and as many as ye shall find, bid to the marriage.

Luke 14:23 And the lord said unto the servant, **<u>Go out into the highways and hedges, and compel *them* to come in</u>**, that my house may be filled.

4

The Desire and Request by Others to Receive Witnessing

You might be surprised to know that there are people in our world that actually want to hear the gospel and want you to come to their door. They are rare but they are there. You may have to go through hundreds to get to one, but they are out there, and it will be worth it. Notice the following examples from the Bible.

A Man in Hell Wanted Someone to Go and Witness to His Five Surviving Brothers

Luke 16:22 And it came to pass, that the beggar died, and was carried by the angels into Abraham's bosom: the rich man also died, and was buried; **Luke 16:23** And in hell he lift up his eyes, being in torments, and seeth Abraham afar off, and Lazarus in his bosom. **Luke 16:24** And he cried and said, Father Abraham, have mercy on me, and send Lazarus, that he may dip the tip of his finger in water, and cool my tongue; for I am tormented in this flame. **Luke 16:25** But Abraham said, Son, remember that thou in thy lifetime receivedst thy good things, and likewise Lazarus evil things: but now he is comforted, and thou art tormented. **Luke 16:26** And beside all this, between us and you there is a great gulf fixed: so that they which would pass from hence to you cannot; neither can they pass to us, that *would come* from thence. **Luke 16:27** <u>Then he said, I pray thee therefore, father, that thou wouldest send him to my father's house:</u> **Luke 16:28** <u>For I have five brethren; that he may testify unto them, lest they also come into this place of torment.</u>

I cannot imagine the agony of any one in hell. As a believer, we must do everything we can by the grace of God to answer their requests for reaching their loved ones. It would literally give a person in Hell some comfort knowing that their loved ones will not be in Hell with them but will go to heaven instead. Most every living believer has lost relatives that have died and because of their unbelief and rejecting Christ, they are cast eternally into Hell. Most every unbeliever has lost relatives that have died and because of their unbelief are cast eternally into Hell. According to the scripture reference above, one of the unbeliever's heart felt requests is for someone to go to their relatives that are still alive and witness to them that they might be saved lest they also come into that place of torment called hell.

Those in Heaven that Want People on Earth to Get Saved

Luke 15:7 I say unto you, that likewise **joy shall be in heaven over one sinner that repenteth,** more than over ninety and nine just persons, which need no repentance.

Luke 15:10 Likewise, I say unto you, **there is joy in the presence of the angels of God over one sinner that repenteth.**

I am sure that there are believers already in heaven that are anxious for the unbelievers they know and are kin to back on Earth to hear the gospel and get saved.

A Man on Earth wanting Someone to Come Help Give out the Gospel

(The Macedonian Call)

Acts 16:9 And a vision appeared to Paul in the night; There stood a man of Macedonia, and prayed him, saying, **Come over into Macedonia, and help us. Acts 16:10** And after he had seen the vision, immediately we endeavoured to go into Macedonia, assuredly gathering that **the Lord had called us for to preach the gospel unto them.**

Another desire and request is coming from people that are still alive on this planet. There are people that are out there in this world that have a desire and request for someone to come to them and tell them how to be saved so they can go to heaven when they die.

Consider the Man in the Bible Called Cornelius

Acts 10:1 <u>There was a certain man in Caesarea called Cornelius</u>, a centurion of the band called the Italian *band*, **Acts 10:2 <u>*A* devout *man*, and one that feared God with all his house, which gave much alms to the people, and prayed to God alway.</u> Acts 10:3** He saw in a vision evidently about the ninth hour of the day an angel of God coming in to him, and saying unto him, Cornelius. **Acts 10:4** And when he looked on him, he was afraid, and said, What is it, Lord? And he said unto him, Thy prayers and thine alms are come up for a memorial before God. **Acts 10:5** And now send men to Joppa, and **<u>call for *one* Simon, whose surname is Peter</u>**: **Acts 10:6** He lodgeth with one Simon a tanner, whose house is by the sea side: **<u>he shall tell thee what thou oughtest to do.</u> Acts 10:7** And when the angel which spake unto Cornelius was departed, he called two of his household servants, and a devout soldier of them that waited on him continually; **Acts 10:8** And when he had declared all *these* things unto them, he sent them to Joppa.

It is interesting that Cornelius actually was given a very good and positive description of his own character and lifestyle. He was devout and he feared God with all his house and he also gave much alms to people and prayed to God always. However, he was visited by an angel which told him to send for Peter. Peter would tell him what he ought to do.

Something was missing. Something was not right. In spite of the wonderful character description, something was wrong.

Farther down in Acts chapter 10, Peter comes to see him. Notice the following passages.

Acts 10:21 Then Peter went down to the men which were sent unto him from Cornelius; and said, Behold, I am he whom ye seek: what *is* the cause wherefore ye are come? **Acts 10:22** And they said, <u>**Cornelius the centurion, a just man, and one that feareth God, and of good report among all the nation of the Jews, was warned from God by an holy angel to send for thee into his house, and to hear words of thee.**</u>

Again, notice the description of Cornelius' character. He was a just man, and feared God, and he had a good report among all the Jews. Notice what the Bible says next. The angel that visited him warned him. You have got to wonder why? What is missing? What is wrong with Cornelius?

As you continue reading you find out that Cornelius was told to send for Peter.

Acts 10:31 And said, Cornelius, thy prayer is heard, and thine alms are had in remembrance in the sight of God. **Acts 10:32** Send therefore to Joppa, and call hither Simon, whose surname is Peter; he is lodged in the house of *one*

Simon a tanner by the sea side: **who, when he cometh, shall speak unto thee.**

Peter has information that Cornelius needs. There is information that Cornelius does not have which is extremely important.

Notice in Acts chapter 11 it is revealed what is missing in Cornelius' life.

Acts 11:13 And he shewed us how he had seen an angel in his house, which stood and said unto him, Send men to Joppa, and call for Simon, whose surname is Peter; **Acts 11:14 Who shall tell thee words, whereby thou and all thy house shall be saved.**

Cornelius was very religious and had a very good reputation, but Cornelius was lost. As religious as Cornelius was, he knew something was missing. God sent an angel to him to call for Peter that he might hear the gospel and trust Christ as his personal Savior. Notice in the following passages some of what Peter told Cornelius.

Acts 10:36 The word which *God* sent unto the children of Israel, preaching **peace by Jesus Christ: (he is Lord of all:) Acts 10:37** That word, *I say*, ye know, which was published throughout all Judaea, and began from Galilee, after the baptism which John preached; **Acts 10:38** How **God anointed Jesus of Nazareth with the Holy Ghost and with power: who went about doing good, and healing all that were oppressed of the devil; for God**

was with him. **Acts 10:39** And we are witnesses of all things which he did both in the land of the Jews, and in Jerusalem; whom **they slew and hanged on a tree: Acts 10:40 Him God raised up the third day, and shewed him openly; Acts 10:41** Not to all the people, but unto witnesses chosen before of God, *even* to us, who did eat and drink with him after he rose from the dead. **Acts 10:42** And he commanded us to preach unto the people, and to testify that **it is he which was ordained of God *to be* the Judge of quick and dead. Acts 10:43** To him give all the prophets witness, that **through his name whosoever believeth in him shall receive remission of sins**.

Believers need to be aware that there are individuals all around us that are open to the gospel of Jesus Christ and some of them are very religious people. We need to be on the alert to share the gospel with everyone we possibly can and everyone that will allow us to do so.

1Pet 3:15 But sanctify the Lord God in your hearts: and ***be* ready always to *give* an answer to every man** that asketh you a reason of the hope that is in you with meekness and fear:

5

Getting into the Mechanics of Witnessing

First the Questions

After approaching the front door of the home, you are visiting and after a brief introduction and a brief conversation, it is time to pin-point some questions to the one that you are talking to and to whom you are about to witness.

> Question #1: Do you go to church anywhere? And if they say no, ask:
>
> Question #2: Do you have a church background? Or, did you use to go to church?

If the individual says yes, ask them the name of their church. Being familiar with this gives you some idea about some of the things they might have been taught in the past. If they say no you still want to go to question #3.

You are not asking these questions just to be making conversation. You want to find out as much as possible about the person's religious background or if they have any religious background at all.

Now you have opportunity to ask question #3.

> Question #3: Do you have the assurance that you will go to heaven when you die are do you have any idea?

Please listen carefully to their answer and how they respond. Watch carefully the expression upon their face.

The answers obviously will vary anywhere from <u>yes</u> to <u>no</u> to <u>I have no idea</u> to <u>I hope so</u> or to some other response like "don't nobody know that."

Now, you have opportunity to ask question #4.

> Question #4: What exactly are you depending on to get you to heaven? Or what do you think it takes to get a person to heaven?

Please listen carefully to their response and let them elaborate as much as they will. Do not jump in too soon and never put words in their mouth. If they mention that they are depending on baptism or church membership or the deeds that they do or having a good lifestyle, let them go on and listen to them carefully to what they say because you are going to need to remind them of what they have said at this point later in the gospel presentation.

Now Getting into the Scriptures

Question #5: If you would allow me to, I have a New Testament with me and I can show you from the Bible what God says we should depend on to get us to heaven. The Bible plainly declares that we can know that we are going to heaven before we die. Are you interested?

If they say no, ask them if you could leave them a gospel track. Give them the track and encourage them to read it and go on to the next door.

If they say yes, take out your New Testament and proceed to show them the following verses and explanations or similar verses to these. You can use as I am about to, much of what you see in Chapter One of this book.

As you begin to share the scriptures with the individual, be careful not to throw to much information at them at one time. Perhaps you have heard the expression, it is difficult to drink from a fire hose. You must be thorough but also concise. Be sure to explain each passage that you share with the individual.

Now, let us begin. Typically, I will at this time read to them **I John 5:13**.

1John 5:13 These things have I written unto you that believe on the name of the Son of God; **that ye may know that ye have eternal life**, and that ye may believe on the name of the Son of God.

After reading the verse I tell them, now let me show you what it means to believe on the name of the Son of God. I usually start from here with telling them that there are two things that God wants you to know beyond even a shadow of a doubt that you actually already know. The third is the one that I will show you that most people do not believe. Many people think that there is no way you can know you are going to heaven before you die. Notice the first thing you already know in this verse.

Rom 3:10 As it is written, There is none righteous, no, not one:

The word, "righteous" means perfect. So, what is the Bible saying here? No one is perfect. You already know that no one is perfect and that you are not perfect. No one has to sell you on this. This is not news to you because you already know this. There is no doubt in your mind about this.

The next verse tells us why we are not perfect. (Now, read the following verse.)

Rom 3:23 For all have sinned, and come short of the glory of God;

This is why we are not perfect because we know that we have sinned against God. This is a warning from God. We have broken God's commandments, and this puts us in extreme danger.

Now the second thing that God wants you to know that you already know is in the following verse.

Romans 6:23 For the wages of sin [is] death...

You already know that someday you will die. Everybody will die someday. You know beyond a shadow of doubt that you will die someday. If we have a choice in the matter, everyone usually picks old age. It has been said that you are not ready to live until you are ready to die. We do not want to be like the fellow that has a hole in the roof of his house. The only time he thinks about fixing the hole in the roof is while it is raining.

Now, the next verse I will show you goes into more detail about what happens to us when we die. In this verse are names of different sins. Some you will understand and some you will not understand. After that, the verse tells us all what we deserve and what happens to us when we die.

Revelation 21:8 But the fearful, and unbelieving, and the abominable, and murderers, and whoremongers, and sorcerers, and idolaters, and <u>**all liars, shall have their part in the lake which burneth with fire and brimstone: which is the second death.**</u>

It only takes one lie to be a liar. Another word for the phrase "the lake which burneth with fire and brimstone" is Hell. Nobody in their right mind wants to go to Hell when they die. However, this is what God says that we all deserve.

You must understand you are **HELPLESS** when it comes to you saving yourself from going to Hell when you die. There is nothing you can do to pay for your own sin.

Understand when I say HELPLESS it means you cannot surrender your life to Christ for salvation. You have no life to surrender. You are dead in trespasses and sins. You cannot yet make Jesus the Lord of your life because you have no life. Jesus will not be Lord of your life until He is Savior of your soul. You cannot turn from your sins because you are dead in your sins. You must see yourself HELPLESS at the Mercy of God.

However, there is good news because God gives us the only way out of this condemnation.

Now, go back to **Rom 6:23** and finish the verse.

Rom 6:23 For the wages of sin *is* death; but **the gift of God *is* eternal life through Jesus Christ our Lord.**

God is offering you eternal life as a gift of God. Eternal life is a free gift. You cannot work for it. We do not earn it or deserve it. Eternal life is living for ever or going to heaven when you die.

Many times, I share a personal illustration from my childhood and it goes as follows.

I thought as a young kid that at the time of my death God would have great big scales up in heaven and he would place all my good deeds on one side of the scale and all my bad deeds on the other side of the scale. If it tilted towards the good, I would go to heaven. If it tilted toward the bad, I would go to hell. The only problem with that is that all the good deeds you have done in your whole life will not pay for even one sin that you have done.

Now, notice what the Bible says in these verses.

Ephesians 2:8 For by grace are ye saved through faith; and that not of yourselves: it is the gift of God: **9** Not of works, lest any man should boast.

Titus 3:5 Not by works of righteousness which we have done, but according to his mercy he saved us, by the washing of regeneration, and renewing of the Holy Ghost;

Galatians 2:16 Knowing that a man is not justified by the works of the law, but by the faith of Jesus Christ, even we have believed in Jesus Christ, that we might be justified by the faith of Christ, and not by the works of the law: for by the works of the law shall no flesh be justified.

Here is where you need to tactfully remind the individual that you are witnessing to, what they told you that they are depending on to get them to heaven earlier. They must see the contrast between what they are depending on (their lifestyle and the deeds that they do) and what they should depend on (Jesus and His death on the cross and burial and resurrection) to get them to heaven. Here is where they must repent or change their mind and agree with the Bible on what they should depend on to get them to heaven.

Make sure you explain carefully who Jesus is and why Jesus died on the cross. At this point would be a good time to ask them, before you show them, why they think that Jesus died.

Before I show you, tell me in your own words why you think Jesus died on the cross?

They may have no idea, or they may have some idea.

Listen to them carefully and then proceed to show them the following passages.

Romans 5:8 But God commendeth his love toward us, in that, **while we were yet sinners, Christ died for us**. **Rom 5:9 Much more then, being now justified by his blood, we shall be saved from wrath through him**. **Rom 5:10** For **if, when we were enemies, we were reconciled to God by the death of his Son, much more, being reconciled, we shall be saved by his life.**

Jesus literally died on the cross to save you and me from going to Hell when we die. Jesus was buried and rose again the third day. This does not mean that everyone will automatically go to heaven. Each person must put their trust and faith in Jesus and what He did on the cross to save them. Now show him the following.

Rom 10:9 That if thou shalt confess with thy mouth the Lord Jesus, and shalt believe in thine heart that God hath raised him from the dead, thou shalt be saved.

Rom 10:10 For with the heart man believeth unto righteousness; and with the mouth confession is made unto salvation.

Getting the Lost Sinner to Ask Jesus to Be Their Savior

Continue to read them the following.

Romans 10:13 For whosoever shall call upon the name of the Lord shall be saved.

Rom 10:14 <u>How then shall they call on him in whom they have not believed</u>? and how shall they believe in him of whom they have not heard? and how shall they hear without a preacher?

Remember, if you are depending on church membership, baptism, or the deeds you do, it does no good to call upon Jesus to save you. If you are willing to depend on Jesus alone to save you, then Jesus is anxious to save you when you call upon him.

Now, ask them, "Do you want Jesus to be your personal Savior?"

Remember no one gets saved that does not want to get saved. If they say yes, offer to lead them in a short simple prayer to God. Get them to repeat after you to God something like the following and for your sake ask them to pray this out loud.

Dear Jesus, I know I am a sinner. I know I deserve Hell, but I know that you died on the cross to pay for my sins and to save me from Hell. Please be my Savior and save my soul. I really mean this Lord. In Jesus name, Amen.

Remind them it is not what they do but what Jesus did that gets them to heaven.

Getting the New Believer to Memorize a Few Things

After they have prayed, ask them if they really meant it? If they say yes, ask them if they are willing to shake on it and offer them your hand and shake hands with them.

Now, encourage them to memorize that day's date and here is why. Sept 22, 1974 (give your date you got saved. This one is mine.) I did what you just did, and I memorized when I did it so I would not doubt or forget that I did do it. As well as you know your birthday, memorize this date.

Invite them to come to your church. Give them the answers to two questions they will soon have even if they do not ask them right then.

The one question is, what happens to me when I sin now after I have asked Jesus to be my Savior?

The answer is that the judgment for your sin changed immediately, when you trusted Christ to be your Savior, from Hell to chastisement. Now show them the following verse.

1Cor 11:32 But when we are judged, we are chastened of the Lord, that we should not be condemned with the world.

We believers are chastised or spanked when we do wrong, but the world of unbelievers is condemned to Hell.

The next question is, why should I go to church and obey God?

The answer is that we do not obey God, hoping it will help get us to heaven. You are promised heaven if you meant it when you asked Christ to be your Savior. Show the following verse again.

1John 5:13 These things have I written unto **<u>you that believe on the name of the Son of God; that ye may know that ye have eternal life,</u>** and that ye may believe on the name of the Son of God.

We should go to church and obey God because we love Him.

John 14:15 If ye love me, keep my commandments.

Before you leave, encourage them to study the gospel track and ask them to memorize **John 3:16.**

John 3:16 For God so loved the world, that he gave his only begotten Son, that whosoever believeth in him should not perish, but have everlasting life.

6

A List of Don'ts When It Comes to Witnessing

As important as witnessing is, the believer needs to be aware that there are many things that the believer must not do when soulwinning. Notice the following list below. The listed items are not in any particular order but the soulwinner must be aware of them all.

1) Never get caught up in an argument with the one to whom you are witnessing.

   One of the worst things you can do is fall into the temptation of trying to win an argument instead of trying to win a soul to Christ. If you since that the conversation is headed for an argument, back off. Remember the following passages.

   Prov 15:1 *A soft answer turneth away wrath: but grievous words stir up anger.*

> ***Prov 13:10*** *Only by pride cometh contention: but with the well advised is wisdom.*

2) Be careful not to give the person to whom you are witnessing too much information at one time. Remember that you are probably talking to a lost person.

   Perhaps you have heard of the phrase, you cannot drink from a fire hose. Of course, answer any question that they might have and be thorough and clear with the plan of salvation but keep it as concise as possible. You can overwhelm them with too much information at one time.

> ***Acts 8:30*** *And Philip ran thither to him, and heard him read the prophet Esaias, and said, Understandest thou what thou readest?* ***Acts 8:31*** *And he said,* <u>***How can I, except some man should guide me***</u>*? And he desired Philip that he would come up and sit with him.*

3) Do not get ahead of the one to whom you are witnessing and put words in their mouth.

> ***Prov 18:13*** *He that answereth a matter before he heareth it, it is folly and shame unto him.*

   There is the temptation to lead the person too fast and even start putting words in their mouth. You must not get too anxious and answer the questions you ask for them. Perhaps you have heard in the court room the objection because a lawyer is leading the witness. Some overzealous and overanxious soul winners almost try to get saved for the one to who they are witnessing. This is very wrong. Let the person to whom you are witnessing answer the questions you ask and listen to them very carefully. Allow them to talk and say their peace about each question. When you show them what the Bible says, they will see where they are different from the Bible. This is where repentance comes in. As you show them what the Bible says, tactfully point out what they said to you in the start of your conversation and compare it to what the Bible says. Ask them if they are willing to change their minds and agree with the Bible. When they genuinely agree with the Bible and admit they were wrong, there will be that genuine change of mind or repentance that God wants them to have.

4) Do not ever be rude. There will never be a time to be rude to anyone, but especially those with whom you are witnessing. You must keep your composure at all times. Remember Jesus called Judas Iscariot, "friend."

> ***Matt 26:50*** *And Jesus said unto him,* ***<u>Friend</u>****, wherefore art thou come? Then came they, and laid hands on Jesus, and took him.*

5) Do not assume the one to whom you are witnessing will understand the religious terminology that you use. Explain every religious word and phrase. For example, if you use any of these terms or phrases: (saved; born again; etc.) they might think you mean baptism or joining a church. Make sure you are clear and break it down to the simplest level you can. Perhaps you have heard of the saying. K. I. S. S. Keep It Simple Stupid.

> *1Cor 2:14 But the natural man receiveth not the things of the Spirit of God: for they are foolishness unto him: neither can he know them, because they are spiritually discerned.*

6) Do not force the conversation or force the witness. If the person is not interested, leave a track if they will take it and go on to the next house. I like chocolate but I do not like it rammed down my throat. I am aware that the lost person you are witnessing to will go to Hell when they die if they reject Christ as their Savior, and we do not know when they will die, but you cannot force the issue. You cannot trick them or force them or badger them into getting saved. The lost person must want to get saved. No one goes to heaven that did not want to get saved.

> *Rom 10:9 That if thou shalt confess with thy mouth the Lord Jesus, and **shalt believe in***

*thine **heart** that God hath raised him from the dead, thou shalt be saved. **Rom 10:10 For with the heart man believeth unto righteousness**; and with the mouth confession is made unto salvation.*

7) Do not pray with them for salvation if they are still depending on deeds that they do or have done to get them to heaven. They must denounce any idea of trusting in their own works or their lifestyle for salvation. If they are still depending on baptism to save them, they are still lost. If they are depending on how good they are, they are still lost no matter how many times you pray with them. Notice the following passage.

*Rom 10:13 For **whosoever shall call upon the name of the Lord shall be saved**. Rom 10:14 **How then shall they call on him in whom they have not believed?** and how shall they believe in him of whom they have not heard? and how shall they hear without a preacher?*

Verse 14 makes it clear that it does no good to call on the Lord for salvation if you are **not** depending on the Lord to save you. Too many over anxious soul-winners jump to getting the lost sinner to pray instead of making sure first that they are **not** depending on their deeds they do or the lifestyle that they live for their salvation and second that they are willing to trust Jesus alone for their salvation. Remember, it is not what they do, it is what Jesus did.

8) Do not go into the house of the one you are visiting unless it is a specific visit of someone you already know, and you have a partner with you. The way the world is getting you must be very careful with what kind of environment you put yourself in.

Too many things can go wrong. False accusations can fly, and reputations can get damaged over nothing. Talk to the people at and through the front doorway or out on the front porch or out in the front yard. I have led many souls to Christ in these locations without going inside the home. Remember your reputation is very fragile. Protect it well.

1Thess 5:22 Abstain from all appearance of evil.

7

Unusual Occurrences
at the Front Door

One of the interesting things about going door to door witnessing is some of the unusual occurrences that sometimes happen at the door you are about to knock on. Through the years I have had some very strange things occur. I would like to share with you just a few episodes.

I was going door to door in a nice well-kept neighborhood. I approached the front porch and knocked on the front door. After doing so I glanced down and curled up in a corner next to the door was a snake. The snake was not poisoness, but it obviously startled me. It was some type of black snake. I disturbed the snake and it proceeded to move toward the front door. Then I got concerned that if the person was home and opened the door, the snake would go into the house. I was afraid that they would think that I put the snake there. Can you imagine what would have happened, next? Fortunately, no one was home and that was one time that I was glad that no one was home. I carefully reached over the snake and put a gospel track in the door. I gladly went on to the next door.

Perhaps you are familiar with the type of fencing for dogs that is buried just under the ground and the dog wears an electric collar that shocks him when he gets in close contact to the buried fencing. In turn, it keeps the dog inside the invisible fence.

I was in another neighborhood and the houses were fairly close together. After knocking on one door, I made a decision to make a short-cut instead of going down the end of the driveway and on to the next house. I walked across the yard to the next door. I had no idea that I had walked across a buried electric fence. Where there is a buried fence there is a dog with a collar. The dog was on the front porch and asleep. Perhaps you have heard the saying, "let sleeping dogs lay." Well, it was too late. I startled the dog and both of us were scared. Fortunately, with all the barking going on the owner came out and got control of the dog. I witnessed to the lady and gave her a track, but It broke me from cutting short-cuts like that through people's yards.

In another instance, I was door-knocking in a duplex and apartment subdivision. As I was going door to door, I noticed a fairly large dog running around in the neighborhood. The dog was not mean and did not even bark at me. He was a happy tail-wagging dog just running through the neighborhood. He was some type of Irish Setter. It was sort of following me. As I approached a door and knocked on it, a lady came to the door and opened it. When she did, the dog went bounding into her house. I ask the lady if that was her dog. She said, "No!" A few seconds later the dog came bounding out into the yard again still wagging his tail. I reassured the lady that it was not my dog, and fortunately she took the moment well and I was able to witness to her and invite her to church.

In another instance, I knocked on the front door to a house in an average neighborhood, and the door opened. Standing in the doorway was a little boy, maybe 2 or 3 years old, that was wearing nothing but a very large smile. The mother came quickly to the door and grabbed her son and covered him. Being very red-faced and obviously embarrassed, she explained that she was trying to give him a bath. She said that there was a knock at the door and her son came running to the door. I gave her a track and invited her to church and went on to the next door.

In another instance, this time I was with a partner. We were going door to door in a very nice neighborhood out in the country. We knocked on one door and talked briefly unto them and gave them a track. They had a Doberman Pincher in a fence in the back yard that was barking very loudly. We started on to the next door and the dog came over the top of the fence. By this time, we were out of their yard and going down the street to the next house. That did not matter. Here came the dog so we made sure not to turn our backs to the dog as we kept slowly walking to the next house. We were both too old to run. The owner of the dog finally came out to get the dog, but the dog ignored the owner and consistently came at us barking and snapping at us. With all the excitement I notice that even though the dog was big, he was also young. I got the impression that the dog was playing with us. This might have been wishful thinking. The owner came closer to us and his dog and I have a hard time believing what I did next. The dog being very close to us, turned his back to us and was looking at his owner. I reached down and got ahold of his collar. It was sort of like getting a tiger by the tail. The dog actually calmed down enough for the owner to come and get him. We happily went on to the next houses.

As you yield to God as a believer and become a "fisher on men," you will have your own experiences and create your own memories. Some will be good and some will be not so good however God will be with you through them all.

8

The Snowball Effect

Allow me first of all to explain what I mean by the "Snowball Effect." It occurs when you are witnessing to one and they get saved and then they lead you to many others that also get saved. Allow me to use some episodes from my own life of some soulwinning experiences that turned into snowball effects.

It was back when I was a young man and a young convert at that. I was running a bus route in a small town not too far from a bigger town where my home church was. It was a typical Saturday, and I was going door to door. I came upon a young boy on a bicycle while I was walking down a sidewalk. The young boy asked me what I was doing. I told the young boy that I was picking up children on a church bus and ask him if he would like to ride with us to church on Sunday. He seemed interested and I asked the young boy if he had the assurance that he would go to heaven when he died. His response was, "no sir," but he asked me if I would come to his house and tell him there.

He pointed to the house and I followed him to his house. I stopped at the door and he listened very carefully as I showed him from the Bible how to be saved. He prayed and asked Jesus to be His personal Savior. I never saw that young boy again.

A week or two later I got a message while at church from the young boy's mother. She asked me to come to her house and talk. When I got to her home, there was a neighbor lady, and the boy's older sister with her in the living room. She told me some horrible news. Her son was out riding his bike down the road and was hit by a vehicle and killed. Then she preceded to tell me before the horrible accident at an earlier date that her son had talked to me and that he had trusted Christ as his Savior and was quite excited about what he had done.

She asked me to tell her what I had told her son because she wanted to be sure that she did what her son had done. I carefully shared the gospel with her and her daughter and neighbor and they all trusted Christ as their Savior.

Days later I got another call. This time it was the young boy's dad. He was a very tall man and very stern looking. I went to the same home again and this time the dad came to the door and invited me in. He was by himself and ask me, "are you the one that talked to my son." I said that I was, and he too asked me what I had told his son.

He too trusted Christ as his Savior after I shared the gospel with him.

God called me to another area, and I heard that the family had come and joined my home church.

This is what I mean by a snowball effect. Allow me to share with you another episode.

This particular episode happened when I was a young pastor in a small town. When I first moved into town different individuals from different places in the town warned me about a man that was very anti-God and hated preachers. They warned me not to go near him or he would probably kill me. The church as usual was very small. Inside that small congregation was a dear lady that would constantly go to the alter at every invitation and she would pray for her husband to get saved. I found out later who her husband was. It was the man that some people warned me about that was anti-God and hated preachers.

After listening to the dear lady pray many times at the alter for many services, I finally got up the nerve to visit the man. Making a long story short after many attempts, I at least was able to talk to him even though he would have nothing to do with God or have any conversation about God. We went fishing together and I helped him skin and butcher deer on Saturday nights.

The day came when God called me to another area, and I thought that I would never see him again. Sometime later,

I got a call from his wife and she said that her husband was very sick and dying with congestive heart failure. Her husband asked her to call me. He would not talk to any other preacher but me. I went to his home and he met me at the door. To make a long story short, we got into to a room together and I shared the gospel with him and he wept very bitterly and asked Christ to be his Savior. He died about six months later and his wife asked me to preach his funeral.

It was a grave side service out in a field. The amazing thing was that the area around the grave site was covered in people. God gave me the opportunity to share the gospel with many people that day who have never been to church. Many of those people trusted Christ as their Savior.

Hopefully, you are seeing what I mean by a snowball effect. Stay faithful at witnessing. Be a faithful fisher of men and God will set you up so that the same type of snowball effect will happen in your life.

Allow me to share another episode. I was in a position in between churches. I was attending and serving at a fairly large church waiting for God to open the next door in my ministry. It was on a Wednesday night service where I was the substitute preaching and teaching from the pulpit. After the service a young man got saved. He was attending faithfully to church and I found out later from his prayer request that his father was very ill and lost and close to death. His father was put in the hospital.

I went to the hospital to visit others that were sick, and I found out where this young man's father was located. I went to his room and witnessed to him. He would have nothing to do with it. Later that same day I walked by his door while going down the hallway. He saw me and asked me to come in and talk to him.

Again, to make a long story short, I shared the gospel with him, and he very sweetly got saved. I believe it was that night that he died. The young son asked me to preach his funeral. It was at a funeral chapel in the large city that the church was in that I was attending at the time. I was not aware that the man that had died was a well-known man in that city. The funeral chapel was packed with people with many that were standing during the service. God again set me up to share the gospel with hundreds of people at one time.

Reader, be faithful to witness one on one with as many people as you possibly can door to door and God will set you up and you too will be able to enjoy the benefits and blessings of the "Snowball Effect."

9

Going By Two's?

I agree whenever possible it is ideal to go door-knocking with a partner. In a time when very few believers are going door to door this can be an extremely rare situation. Do not wait on a partner to go witnessing. You will find that you will rarely go. Allow me to go to some scripture to deal with the subject of going by twos.

Mark 6:7 And he called *unto him* the twelve, and **began to send them forth by two and two**; and gave them power over unclean spirits;

Luke 10:1 After these things the Lord appointed other seventy also, and **sent them two and two** before his face into every city and place, whither he himself would come.

As you can see from the passages above, Jesus was starting with the number of twelve and then seventy and he sent them out two by two. If there is no twelve or no seventy or no two, I do not believe God wants you to stay home and not witness because you do not have a partner. The greatest silent partner there is on the planet is the Holy Spirit. Of the many times in my life of being close to God in preaching or teaching or reading my Bible, or praying, the time that God has been closest to me is when I am going door to door soulwinning.

Now notice some more verses from the Bible.

Acts 8:26 And the angel of the Lord spake unto **Philip**, saying, Arise, and go toward the south unto the way that goeth down from Jerusalem unto Gaza, which is desert. **Acts 8:27** And he arose and went: and, behold, **a man of Ethiopia**, an eunuch of great authority under Candace queen of the Ethiopians, who had the charge of all her treasure, and had come to Jerusalem for to worship, **Acts 8:28** Was returning, and sitting in his chariot read Esaias the prophet. **Acts 8:29** Then the Spirit said unto Philip, Go near, and join thyself to this chariot. **Acts 8:30** And Philip ran thither to *him*, and heard him read the prophet Esaias, and said, Understandest thou what thou readest? **Acts 8:31** And he said, How can I, except some man should guide me? And he desired Philip that he would come up and sit with him. **Acts 8:32** The place of the scripture which he read was this, He was led as a sheep to the slaughter; and like a lamb dumb before his shearer, so opened he not his mouth: **Acts 8:33** In his humiliation his judgment was taken away: and who shall declare his generation? for his life is taken from the earth. **Acts 8:34** And the eunuch answered Philip, and said, I pray thee, of whom speaketh the prophet this? of himself, or of some other man? **Acts 8:35** Then Philip opened his mouth, and began at the same scripture, and preached unto him Jesus.

After reading the above passage you will see that Philip was alone. He had no human partner. Was he to delay the witness and first go find a partner? Of course not! The Holy Spirit was his partner.

I understand it is good to have the opportunity to take someone with you to train them as a silent partner to listen and learn or to have a partner to silently pray as you witness and try to intercept any interferences. I am all for this. So, if there is no one available to train, do you stay at home? In the over 40 years of door-knocking in my life, the percentage of going alone is higher than when I have gone with a partner.

Do not misunderstand me. It is a thrill and a joy to go with another soulwinner or take someone with you to train. However, consider this. If there are two soulwinners, do you not think that they can cover more area if they divide up and go separately rather than going together?

The point is if you have the luxury of having a partner enjoy. If there is no partner, do not let that stop you from going soulwinning.

10

The Drawing of the Holy Spirit

One of the things that has been misunderstood and even used to not go soulwinning is the matter of the drawing of the Holy Spirit and work of the Holy Spirit to convict the lost sinner that he is lost and needs to be saved. Some believers have literally sat at home waiting on the Holy Spirit to draw the lost sinner to be saved. Notice the following verses from the Bible concerning the draw of the Holy Spirit.

John 6:44 <u>No man can come to me, except the Father which hath sent me draw him</u>: and I will raise him up at the last day.

John 12:32 <u>And I, if I be lifted up from the earth, will draw all *men* unto me.</u>

Some believers, as well meaning as they may be, have misunderstood what is involved when it comes to the Holy Spirit drawing sinners to be saved and have used their notion of what it means for an excuse not to go soulwinning. They have totally ignored the commands in the Bible to go to the lost sinner and instead the believer is waiting for the lost sinner to come to church to get the gospel.

Allow me to explain the drawing of the Holy Spirit. When you read **John 6:44**, you might ask how does one know when the Holy Spirit draws people? If you would read **John 12:32**, God tells you when the Holy Spirit draws the lost sinner to be saved. It is when Jesus is lifted up. So, the fair question to ask is when is Jesus lifted up? The answer is when the soulwinner shares the gospel with the lost sinner and the lost sinner hears the truth of the gospel about the death, the burial, and the resurrection of Christ from the soulwinner. Jesus is lifted up and the Holy Spirit draws as the soulwinner shares the truth of the gospel. Be sure not to overlook the phrase in **John 12:32** that says, "will **draw all men** unto me." Notice the following passage.

John 16:7 Nevertheless I tell you the truth; It is expedient for you that I go away: for if I go not away, the Comforter will not come unto you; but if I depart, I will send him unto you. **John 16:8** And when he is come, **he will reprove the world of sin**, and **of righteousness, and of judgment**: **John 16:9** **Of sin, because they believe not on me; John 16:10** Of righteousness, because I go to my Father, and ye see me no more; **John 16:11** Of judgment, because the prince of this world is judged.

Notice the passage that says that the Holy Spirit will reprove the world of sin. Notice that sin has no "S" on the end of it. Sin in this passage is singular. The sin is the sin of unbelief. Notice in **John 16:9** "of sin, because they believe not on me." The soul-winner needs to be reminded that the Holy Spirit deals with one sin alone when it comes to the lost sinner. It is the sin of unbelief. No matter what other sins the lost sinner is involved in, the soul-winner must stay focused on the sin of unbelief. You are not there to reform the lost sinner. You are there to give the gospel to the lost sinner so the lost sinner can be saved.

11

Some False Teachings that have Hindered and even Halted the Drive to go Soul-Winning in Many Churches and with Many Believers

Distortion of Repentance

In many fundamental Bible believing churches, the teaching and understanding of repentance has gotten totally distorted. I have noticed that the churches that believe that repentance means for the lost sinners to turn from their sins before they can trust Christ as their Savior, loses their drive to go soulwinning typically to the point of drying up to a slow drip and eventually stopping.

Do not misunderstand me, if the believer is not accurate on presenting the plan of salvation, I do not believe they need to be out witnessing anyway. They need to get salvation straight first for the sake of themselves as well as for others to whom they will witness.

This author has written another book entitled, "How to study the Bible for Yourself." At the end of that book is a very detailed study on what the Bible says about "Repentance." I have put a small section of that study in the portion of this book just ahead. Notice the following.

2Cor 7:8 For though I made you sorry with a letter, **I do not repent**, **though I did repent**: for I perceive that the same epistle hath made you sorry, though *it were* but for a season. **2Cor 7:9** Now I rejoice, not that ye were made sorry, but that **ye sorrowed to repentance**: for ye were made sorry after a godly manner, that ye might receive damage by us in nothing. **2Cor 7:10** For **godly sorrow worketh repentance to salvation not to be repented of:** but the sorrow of the world worketh death.

Rom 11:29 For **the gifts and calling of God *are* without repentance**.

Heb 7:21 (For those priests were made without an oath; but this with an oath by him that said unto him, **The Lord sware and will not repent**, Thou *art* a priest for ever after the order of Melchisedec:)

Now allow me to make a brief comment about each passage from above.

(II Cor 7:8) "I do not repent, though I did repent." Surely, we can see that the word, repent, does not me "turn from sin." Allow me to inject the false definition of repent in this phrase. "I do not turn from sin, though I did turn from sin." Are we to think that Paul would not turn from sin, though he did turn from sin. Now allow me to inject the correct definition of the word, repent, in this phrase. "I do not change my mind, though I did change my mind."

(II Cor 7:9) "Ye sorrowed to repentance." First of all, here Paul is addressing saved people not lost people. Secondly, this passage proves that sorrow for sin and repentance are not the same. Lastly, the individuals Paul addressed sorrowed to the changing of their minds.

(II Cor. 7:10) "Godly sorrow worketh repentance to salvation." This passage also proves again that sorrow and repentance are not the same. Again, allow me to inject the false definition of the word, repentance, into the passage. "Godly sorrow worketh turning from sin to salvation not to be turning from your sin." This does not make since with using this definition. Now, we will inject the correct definition of the word, repent, in the passage. "Godly sorrow worketh changing of your mind to salvation not to be changing your mind from." The change of mind that every lost sinner must have is changing their mind to believing the Bible is the word of God, believing that Jesus is the Son of God, and His death on the cross is the only thing that pays for his sin. The lost sinner must change his mind about depending on himself and the deeds he is doing to get him to heaven to believing that Jesus alone is the only one that will promise him heaven by trusting Christ as his own personal Savior.

(Rom 11:29) "the gifts and calling of God *are* without repentance." Now, allow me to inject the false definition of the word, repent, into the passage. "The gifts and calling of God are without "turning from sin." You are surely not foolish enough to believe that it is the correct definition of the word, repent. Now, allow me to inject the true definition of the word, repent, into the passage. "The gifts and calling of God are without "changing your mind."

(Hebrews 7:21) "The Lord sware and will not repent." Now allow me to inject the false definition of the word, repent, in the passage. "The Lord sware and will not "turn from sin." Obviously, you can see how blasphemous the wrong definition of the word, repent, would be in this passage. Are we really to think that the Lord has any sin to turn from? Now, for the correct definition of the word, repent, to be injected into the passage. "The Lord sware and will not change His mind."

Allow me also to make this as clear as I can. If the individual is depending on turning from his sins to get him to heaven instead Jesus and His death, burial, and resurrection to get him to heaven, he is lost. Even if he calls himself a fundamental preacher.

As I said before, if you do not have the plan of salvation straight in your mind, you need to study until you get it straight. You have no business going out door to door yet.

Remember a bogged down truck cannot pull out a bogged down truck. I will leave this point with this warning.

Gal 1:8 But <u>**though we, or an angel from heaven, preach any other gospel unto you than that which we have preached unto you, let him be accursed**</u>.

Gal 1:9 As we said before, so say I now again, <u>**If any *man* preach any other gospel unto you than that ye have received, let him be accursed.**</u>

Some form of Calvinism

Another false teaching that has crept into many churches and into some believers' heads, is that getting saved is virtually automatic. "Whatever will be, will be." If the believer does think it is automatic on the matter of people getting saved, they will stay at home and forget about any commandment that God gives from the Bible to go into all the world. Please see this author's book on "Anti-Calvinism."

It is true that God will use another believer to give out the gospel if the former believer has found a salve for his conscious to not witness even to his own blood kin. That former believer will learn more about the chastening hand of God first-hand.

The Slander Meant by the Term, "Easy Believism"

Jas 2:19 Thou believest that there is one God; thou doest well: the devils also believe, and tremble.

It is interesting that clear back to the 1500's that the false prophets were using **James 2:19** against believers, who were about to be put to death for their faith, trying to change the believers from depending on Jesus to save them to depending on their own works and deeds that they do to save them.

First, allow me to explain that just believing there is one God is a far cry from believing the gospel of Jesus Christ. Just because a person believes there is one God does not mean that they are saved.

For many years the Armenian religions (That is people who believe you can lose your salvation.) have used the term "easy-believism" to mock the believers that teach that "for by grace are ye saved through faith in Jesus and His death, burial, and resurrection and that teach eternal security." Now there are people that say they believe in eternal security but are using the same label, "easy-believism," to poke fun of and mock believers that correctly teach repentance and eternal security. We have come a long way in the wrong direction. How sad!

I am aware of some that are out trying to witness that jump ahead and tell the lost sinner to "one two three pray after me" and you are saved. If you will revisit Chapter

5 in this book you will see a detailed presentation on giving out the gospel. This presentation is a far cry from "one two three pray after me" and you are saved by just believing that there is one God.

Notice the following passages about little children.

Matt 19:14 But Jesus said, **Suffer little children, and forbid them not, to come unto me: for of such is the kingdom of heaven.**

Mark 10:14 But when Jesus saw *it*, he was much displeased, and said unto them, **Suffer the little children to come unto me, and forbid them not: for of such is the kingdom of God.**

Luke 18:16 But Jesus called them *unto him*, and said, **Suffer little children to come unto me, and forbid them not: for of such is the kingdom of God.**

Matt 18:3 And said, Verily I say unto you, **Except ye be converted, and become as little children, ye shall not enter into the kingdom of heaven**.

Mark 10:15 Verily I say unto you, **Whosoever shall not receive the kingdom of God as a little child, he shall not enter therein.**

Luke 18:17 Verily I say unto you, **Whosoever shall not receive the kingdom of God as a little child shall in no wise enter therein.**

Matt 18:4 <u>Whosoever therefore shall humble himself as this little child, the same is greatest in the kingdom of heaven</u>.

The person that mocks at those who are genuine fishers of men with the slander of "easy believism" needs to be aware that there is nothing hard about the gospel of Jesus Christ. It was designed for little children as well as adults as you can see from the passages above. It is not supposed to be hard to believe on Jesus Christ and trust him as your personal Savior. The individuals who are slinging the slander of "easy-believism" are putting themselves in some very bad company.

Mark 10:15 Verily I say unto you, **<u>Whosoever shall not receive the kingdom of God as a little child, he shall not enter therein.</u>**

You will notice that the passage above does not say, "whosoever shall not receive the kingdom of God **<u>as an adult</u>**, he shall not enter therein."

It is not supposed to be hard to believe on Jesus Christ and trust him as your personal Savior. The individuals who are slinging the slander of "easy-believism" are putting themselves in some very bad company.

What makes it difficult is when the lost sinner gets it in his head to depend on other things to get them to heaven besides Jesus and what He did for them on the cross. For example, a person that is depending on turning from their sins for salvation instead of depending on Jesus for salvation is lost.

The False Teaching of Lordship Salvation

Thinking that you should make Jesus the Lord of your life for salvation instead of trusting Christ as Savior for salvation has been nick-named "Lordship Salvation." The lost sinner is trying to depend on their own surrender instead of the Savior Jesus Christ for their salvation. Notice the following passages.

Matt 7:22 <u>**Many will say to me in that day**</u>, <u>**Lord, Lord**</u>, have we not prophesied in thy name? and in thy name have cast out devils? and in thy name done many wonderful works?

Matt 7:23 And then will I profess unto them, <u>**I never knew you: depart from me, ye that work iniquity.**</u>

1Cor 12:3 Wherefore I give you to understand, that no man speaking by the Spirit of God calleth Jesus accursed: and <u>***that* no man can say that Jesus is the Lord, but by the Holy Ghost.**</u>

Of the many things that the passage above is telling us, one of the things is that a lost person does not have the Holy Ghost and so a lost person cannot make Jesus the Lord of their life due to the absence of the Holy Ghost.

The Mistake of Trying to Reform an Unbeliever Instead of Getting them to Trust Christ

Some misguided individuals make the attempt of trying to get lost sinners to clean up their life before they can get saved. The sinner being witnessed to must focus on one sin and one sin alone. That focus must be on the horrible sin of "unbelief." This is the sin that takes mankind to Hell. Notice the following passage.

John 16:7 Nevertheless I tell you the truth; It is expedient for you that I go away: for if I go not away, the Comforter will not come unto you; but if I depart, I will send him unto you. **John 16:8** And when he is come, **he will reprove the world of sin**, and of righteousness, and of judgment: **John 16:9 Of sin, because they believe not on me**; **John 16:10** Of righteousness, because I go to my Father, and ye see me no more; **John 16:11** Of judgment, because the prince of this world is judged.

According to the passage above the Holy Spirit will convict a lost sinner of only one sin when it comes to Salvation. The sin is unbelief.

Some misguided individuals make the mistake of bringing up other sins in a person's life that they need to clean up. What other sins that a lost sinner is involved in at this point is totally irrelevant. Do they need to stop smoking before they can get saved? Do they need to stop drinking before they get saved? Do they need to give up drugs before they get saved? The answer to all these questions is no. Of course, the lost sinner must have a clear mind in order to hear the gospel. However, if you tell a lost sinner that he must do these things first and if he has some form of success in doing so, he will be depending on himself and what he did instead of Jesus and what Jesus did for his salvation. Allow me to end this point with the following passages.

John 3:18 He that believeth on him is not condemned: but **he that believeth not is condemned already, because he hath not believed in the name of the only begotten Son of God.**

John 3:36 He that believeth on the Son hath everlasting life: and **he that believeth not the Son shall not see life; but the wrath of God abideth on him.**

12

The Leading of the Holy Spirit

One of the things that is priceless for the soul-winner is the leading of the Holy Spirit. The thrilling truth about this is that because a person has trusted Christ as their Savior, that person is promised to be led by the Holy Spirit. Notice the following passage.

Rom 8:14 For as many as are led by the Spirit of God, they are the sons of God.

Everyone that wants to become a fisher of men must be sensitive to the leading of the Holy Spirit. This is one of the benefits of staying as close to God as you can.

Notice below a few passages from the Book of Acts that show us how God led God's people in witnessing.

Philip and the Ethiopian Eunuch

Acts 8:26 And <u>**the angel of the Lord spake unto Philip, saying, Arise, and go toward the south unto the way that goeth down from Jerusalem unto Gaza, which is desert**</u>.

Acts 8:29 <u>**Then the Spirit said unto Philip, Go near, and join thyself to this chariot**</u>.

The Spirit Guiding Philip

Acts 8:39 And when they were come up out of the water, <u>**the Spirit of the Lord caught away Philip,**</u> that the eunuch saw him no more: and he went on his way rejoicing.

Ananias to Saul who became Paul

Acts 9:10 And there was a certain disciple at Damascus, named Ananias; <u>**and to him said the Lord in a vision, Ananias.**</u> And he said, Behold, I *am here*, Lord. **Acts 9:11** And <u>**the Lord *said* unto him, Arise, and go into the street which is called Straight, and enquire in the house of Judas for *one* called Saul, of Tarsus: for, behold, he prayeth**</u>, **Acts 9:12** And hath seen in a vision a man named Ananias coming in, and putting *his* hand on him, that he might receive his sight. **Acts 10:19** While Peter thought on the vision, <u>**the Spirit said unto him, Behold, three men seek thee.**</u> **Acts 10:20**

Arise therefore, and get thee down, and go with them, doubting nothing: for I have sent them.

Sometimes the Holy Spirit Forbids us to Go to Certain Areas Because it is not the Right Time

Acts 16:6 Now when they had gone throughout Phrygia and the region of Galatia, and **were forbidden of the Holy Ghost to preach the word in Asia**, **Acts 16:7** After they were come to Mysia, **they assayed to go into Bithynia: but the Spirit suffered them not**. **Acts 16:8** And they passing by Mysia came down to Troas.

The Call to Macedonia

Acts 16:9 And a vision appeared to Paul in the night; There stood a man of Macedonia, and prayed him, saying, **Come over into Macedonia, and help us**. **Acts 16:10** And after he had seen the vision, immediately we endeavoured to go into Macedonia, **assuredly gathering that the Lord had called us for to preach the gospel unto them**.

The Personal Leading of the Holy Spirit

This author deems it necessary to remind the believer at this point that the Bible, the Word of God, is the sole and final authority for faith and practice. God will never lead you contrary to the Word of God and God will never lead you to contradict the Word of God.

Ask God for Guidance

Proverbs 3:5 <u>Trust in the LORD with all thine heart; and lean not unto thine own understanding.</u> **3:6** <u>In all thy ways acknowledge him, and he shall direct thy paths.</u>

You Are Not Asking God for a Sign, You are Asking God for Guidance

Isaiah 7:10 Moreover <u>the LORD spake</u> again unto Ahaz, saying, **11** <u>Ask thee a sign of the LORD thy God; ask it either in the depth, or in the height above.</u> **12** But Ahaz said, <u>I will not ask, neither will I tempt the LORD.</u>

God will Establish the Right thoughts and Guidance in your Mind

Proverbs 16:1 The preparations of the heart in man, and the answer of the tongue, [is] from the LORD. **16:2** All the ways of a man [are] clean in his own eyes; but the LORD weigheth the spirits. **16:3** <u>Commit thy works unto the LORD, and thy thoughts shall be established</u>.

Do not Follow your own Heart, Follow God's Word

Prov 28:26 <u>He that trusteth in his own heart is a fool</u>: but whoso walketh wisely, he shall be delivered.

Ps 119:133 <u>Order my steps in thy word: and let not any iniquity have dominion over me.</u>

Do not Confuse Your Thoughts
with God's Thoughts

Isa 55:8 For my thoughts *are* not your thoughts, neither *are* your ways my ways, saith the LORD. **Isa 55:9** For *as* the heavens are higher than the earth, so are my ways higher than your ways, and my thoughts than your thoughts.

With the above verses to back you up, we must be as sensitive as we possibly can to the leading of the Holy Spirit in all things in life but especially when it comes to soulwinning. Ask God to direct your thoughts and your steps that you might be in the right place at the right time and say the right thing the right way.

13

Pray to be a Triple A Soulwinner

This author prays before each time he goes out witnessing for God to make him a triple "A" soulwinner. Allow me to explain. There are characteristics I pray for when I am about to go soulwinning. Each starts with an "A." They are as follows.

A #1 Alert:

One of the things I ask God for when it comes to witnessing is that I ask God to make me alert to the leading of the Holy Spirit. I ask God to make me sensitive to the leading of the Holy Spirit. I must know from God, where to visit, when to visit, and who to visit. I must be sensitive and submissive to God's guidance. I must stay alert to God's leading hand. I pray that I will also be submissive to the leading of the Holy Spirit. When God makes known to me what I should do, then I must do it. When God makes known to me what I should say, then I must say it. When God makes known to me where I should go, there I must go there. Remember because we are saved, we are promised to be led by the Holy Spirit. Notice the following passage.

Rom 8:14 For as many as are led by the Spirit of God, they are the sons of God.

A #2 Affective:

Another thing I ask God for when it comes to witnessing is to make me affective in my witnessing to others. I regularly ask God to help me **say the right thing at the right time in the right way**. I ask God to please not let me cower down. I asked God that He would grant that I might speak the word of God with boldness and humility but not with arrogance. Notice the following passage.

Acts 4:29 And now, Lord, behold their threatenings: and **grant unto thy servants, that with all boldness they may speak thy word**,

A #3 Active:

Another thing I ask God for when it comes to witnessing is for God to keep me active when it comes to going out witnessing. I pray that God would help me to stay faithful in witnessing and consistent in my witnessing for Christ.

14

God's Divine Providential Guiding Hand

Ps 32:8 <u>I will instruct thee and teach thee in the way which thou shalt go: I will guide thee with mine eye.</u>

Ps 48:14 For this God *is* our God for ever and ever: <u>he will be our guide *even* unto death</u>.

Ps 73:24 <u>Thou shalt guide me with thy counsel, and afterward receive me *to* glory</u>.

One of the things that every believer needs to watch for in their personal life but especially the one that seeks to be a fisher of men is God's providential guiding hand. It is amazing and thrilling to see God work to put things in line with timing and moving obstacles out of the way to clear a path for the believer. The saying is true that I have heard for so long. Where God guides, God provides. Allow me to share with you a few examples of what I mean.

Years ago, I was driving to a section of houses in a rural area and I parked on the side of the road. There were no houses where I parked. I typically look for a spot to park that will not be where someone would come out and ask me to move my vehicle. From there I would walk down the road and go door to door. I typically do not take my vehicle to each driveway. I cannot afford the gas or the wear and tear on my vehicle with the regular starting and stopping. There was an open field there and I thought it would be a good spot to park. For some reason, I could not feel comfortable about it and I got uneasy about parking there. So, I moved my truck across the road and got out and locked the truck and went door-knocking. When I returned to my vehicle, I discovered something quite interesting had occurred while I was gone. The owner to the field had decided to burn off the grass in the field while I was gone. If I had left my truck where I first parked it, the fire would have caught my truck on fire. I was thrilled with God's kind providential hand leading me to move my truck across the road.

In another situation, I was going door-knocking and this time I had a partner with me. In a typical procedure, we would take one road about two blocks long and we would go down the right side to the end and cross the road and come back up the left side, knocking on each door as we went. We had followed this procedure many times in the past. For some reason we started almost in the middle of the block and by the time we were at the last house, it ended in the middle of the block. At that last house, we were about to go to the door and a man pulled up in that driveway. I stopped from going to the house and went to the man that pulled up in his driveway. To make I long story short the man sweetly got saved. As we were leaving, I told my partner that had we followed the usual procedure, when we got to that man's house, he would not have been home and we would have missed him. I was thrilled with God's kind providential hand in timing us to be at that house at just the right time.

In another situation, it was on a Saturday morning. It was raining. I do not mean a drizzle. It was a steady rain. The weatherman said it would be an all-day thing. So, I told my partner that we would wait at our homes. Since the location of where we were going door knocking was close to where we lived, as soon as the rain let up, we would meet in our vehicles and go door to door in our vehicles. That early afternoon the rain let up and I decided to go ahead and visit a few homes. While I was back in my truck, my partner called and said he was also on his way and we met and proceeded to the area to visit. I pulled up next to a home and got out to knock on the door of the home. A young man of 16 years old came out and under the car port of the home I was able to lead him to Christ. I found out that had we went visiting the usual time he would not have been at home. I was thrilled again with God's kind providential hand in timing me to be at that house at just the right time.

There are countless cases like the ones I am sharing with you.

In another situation, this time I was not out visiting door to door. I was working out in my yard and I needed some help to load something in the back of my truck. I have a neighbor that I witnessed to several times. He typically would change the subject or avoid me altogether, but he was a very nice and friendly man. I walked over to his house and asked him to come help me load something in the back of my truck. He happily did so. When we got the equipment loaded, he stayed with me at the back of my truck and started asking me questions about some things that he has never got answers to. I told him that I would give him his answers if he would allow me to share how to be saved with him. He said yes and I was unfortunately caught without a Bible or New Testament. I proceeded to explain how to be saved. He listened carefully for the first time with very important questions that I answered. He told me no one has ever told this to him and no one has had a one on one conversation with him giving him a clear explanation. I urged him to make sure to put his faith in Jesus to save him and not any deeds or lifestyle that he had. He said he agreed with what I told him and that he had been wrong about how to be saved. I asked him when he had gotten it straight in his mind and he said just then.

God providentially used a moment of me asking my neighbor to help with a simple task and my neighbor opened the conversation which allowed me to share the gospel and he got saved. I also answered the other questions that he had, and he was relieved and happy for it. I was not at that time expecting to have the opportunity to witness, but as usual, God set it up again. Several other things got me to this point. My computer was out of order at that moment so I could not work inside. The weather was good, so I started working in my yard. I started loading some equipment in my truck to be removed. I had one piece of equipment that was too heavy for me to load by myself. So, I went to my neighbor who happened to be home and asked him for help. There in a one-on-one conversation the man sweetly trusted Christ as his Savior.

In another episode, I was going door to door, and approached a house with a front porch on it. I noticed a young man sitting on a chair on the front porch. I introduced myself and asked the young man if he lived there. He said no but that he was house sitting for a friend. It was Saturday morning, and I asked him about church and began to witness to him. To make a long story short, he trusted Christ as his Savior. The young man happened to be there on the porch where he did not live, and I happened to come by the house and talk with him. I was thrilled again with God's kind providential hand in timing me to be at that house at just the right time.

One thing I want to encourage every fisher of men to do before they leave to go soulwinning is illustrated in a conversation between Abraham and his servant in the Bible. The servant was asked to go get a bride for his son. Notice the passage below.

Gen 24:7 The LORD God of heaven, which took me from my father's house, and from the land of my kindred, and which spake unto me, and that sware unto me, saying, Unto thy seed will I give this land; **<u>he shall send his angel before thee</u>**, and thou shalt take a wife unto my son from thence.

Gen 24:40 And he said unto me, **<u>The LORD, before whom I walk, will send his angel with thee, and prosper thy way</u>**; and thou shalt take a wife for my son of my kindred, and of my father's house:

Ask God to send his angel before you to prosper each episode of soul winning you go on.

15

Keeping Some Kind of Record of Your Visitation

It is important for you to keep some kind of record of your visitation. There are many benefits for doing so. It helps you keep up with where you have been. It helps you not to leave anyone out. It helps you be consistent with how many visits per week you are making. It also helps you to know where to follow-up with specific visits. If you are a member of a Bible believing church or even a pastor of a Bible believing church you need to get a map of the immediate area of the church and your home. Allow me to share with you what I have done in the past and am doing now.

In the present age of computers, I have gone on the internet to view a map that I have pulled up on the computer of the immediate area that my church and church family are in and then copy and paste that area of the map on to a document into an auto-cad file of the auto-cad program that I already have on my computer. After inserting the cut of the map on to an auto-cad sheet, I then trace the streets and type in the street names. After this is completed, I erase the map insert and what is left is the streets and names of the streets. As I go visiting, I take a copy of the particular street area on an 8 ½ x 11 sheet and put it in a clip-board where I will go door to door visiting. I make a small circle representing each house that I visit along that street. The circle has to be large enough to write a 3 or 4 digit house number in it. As each house is visited, I mark by the circle with a choice of abbreviations depending on the reaction at each home. The abbreviations are typically as follows.

NH for not home; NC for not churched; GV for good visit. Abbreviate the name of the church they go to if any. If the individual gives me a clear testimony that they are saved, I put a S with a circle around it. NI for not interested. BV for a bad visit, and so on. If I lead them to Christ, I put a * by the circle and house number that I am at and on another sheet write their name and age and address.

If you do not have a computer or internet, take a few blank sheets of paper in a clip board and sketch the streets, street names, and house numbers as you go.

When returning to home, if you have a computer, update the file on the computer adding the marks and notes from the visitation.

If you do not have a computer, get a loose leaf note book and keep each sheet that you make in that note book. Sketch the street and name and each house number on that street on the paper in your clipboard.

In my present location, I am able to go through the entire area in 18 to 24 months and then start back through them again. That is about 100 visits per month or about 25 visits each week. This particular area has about 35 subdivisions and growing.

In a separate sheet, I make a spread-sheet and make a list of every subdivision and every street in that subdivision. I set up columns to represent years. In each square in that column, I put the day and month when I visit at that particular subdivision and street. This helps me to know, God willing, where to visit next and to keep up with where I have already been.

In another worksheet, I keep a record of all the visits I have made on that day. This will be added to and updated each time I go visit.

Once you have finished the area, you need to save each sheet or computer file. Remember the map will not change so you will no longer need to sketch a map. You might need to add more circles and house numbers for new homes that are built later.

Something also that I have done long before computers were available. I would write the name of the individual that got saved and their age in the back of the New Testament that I was carrying. I would write the age down to help me remember the person that I led to Christ. This also makes a prayer list for you so you can pray regularly for each person that you have led to Christ.

Please keep some kind of record like this. It will help you to be organized and help you not to miss a house or leave out a house anywhere as you visit. This will also help you see the pace that you are making. It is important to keep up with the pace of how many visits you make per week, per month, and so on.

16

Dealing with Intimidation

A big hurdle that the soulwinner will come up against is intimidation. I will agree that going door to door visiting can be very dangerous. You must pray for safety as you visit and be in fellowship with God. Without God's fellowship and power many things around you can get very intimidating. However, this kind of fear can be used to the soulwinner's advantage to see the need for God's fellowship and power. I will share with you how to do this in this chapter. Allow me first to go to some passages in the Bible.

Acts 4:29 And now, <u>**Lord, behold their threatenings: and grant unto thy servants, that with all boldness they may speak thy word**</u>, **Acts 4:30** By stretching forth thine hand to heal; and that signs and wonders may be done by the name of thy holy child Jesus. **Acts 4:31** And when they had prayed, the place was shaken where they were assembled together; and <u>**they were all filled with**</u>

the Holy Ghost, and they spake the word of God with boldness.

Now, allow me to show you some ways that you can use the fear and intimidation to your advantage. When fear and intimidation are present, there are a few things that are absent. One is faith in God and the other is your love for God and people. Allow me to illustrate my point with the following.

Most everyone that has a vehicle also has a gas gage on the dash of the vehicle that tells you how much gas is in the tank of the vehicle. The gage is very important because it tells you when you need to go to the gas station and refuel. Fear and intimidation are the gas gages and strong indicators that you are running low on faith in God and love for God and people. By being alone with God in prayer and reading your Bible you will be able to refuel. The soulwinner that neglects time alone with God in prayer and Bible study cannot expect to be successful for God in soulwinning and will typically be overcome with fear and intimidation and will lose the desire and thrill of going soulwinning. Let us have a look at the passage that tells us how we get faith.

Rom 10:17 So then faith _cometh_ by hearing, and hearing by the word of God.

Now, notice another passage that tells us that love is stronger than fear.

1John 4:18 <u>**There is no fear in love; but perfect love casteth out fear**</u>: because fear hath torment. He that feareth is not made perfect in love.

We know that we are commanded to love one another and love our enemies. So, if we are being overcome with fear and intimidation, it means we are short on time alone with God in Bible study and in prayer. Notice the following.

Acts 4:13 Now <u>**when they saw the boldness of Peter and John**</u>, and perceived that they were unlearned and ignorant men, they marvelled; and <u>**they took knowledge of them, that they had been with Jesus.**</u>

It is also true that attempting to carry around with us unconfessed sin will cause great problems when it comes to soulwinning. Our communication with God must be constant especially when we are out visiting. Notice the following passages.

Ps 66:18 <u>**If I regard iniquity in my heart, the Lord will not hear *me***</u>:

Isa 59:1 Behold, the LORD'S hand is not shortened, that it cannot save; neither his ear heavy, that it cannot hear: **(Isa 59:2)** But <u>**your iniquities have separated between you and your God, and your sins have hid *his* face from you, that he will not hear.**</u>

Matt 24:12 And <u>because iniquity shall abound, the love of many shall wax cold</u>.

The passage above helps us to see what we can do to strengthen our love for God and for each other. If sin makes your love wax cold, living an obedient life for God makes your love for God and people stronger and warmer.

The bottom line here is you want to keep your tank full of gas.

(1Pet 3:15) But <u>sanctify the Lord God in your hearts</u>: and *be* <u>ready always to *give* an answer to every man that asketh you a reason of the hope that is in you with meekness and fear</u>:

Now, let us take another perspective. I had been soulwinning for a few years when it finally hit me. It occurred to me that the one on the other side of the door that you are about to knock on is typically more intimidated than you are. It is necessary that your love for souls and your concern for them is present to move the fear and intimidation aside in that moment the door is opened and set up the opportunity to share the gospel. The people you are visiting need to know that you really care and keep in mind that they can tell when you do not.

Let us deal with our love for souls. You need to be aware that your love for God is directly connected with your love for people. The more you love God the more you will love people. This is another gage for the believer. Notice the following passage.

(1John 4:20) <u>**If a man say, I love God, and hateth his brother, he is a liar: for he that loveth not his brother whom he hath seen, how can he love God whom he hath not seen?**</u>

If your love for people is lacking, your love for God is also lacking. You will need love and faith from God and in God to function successfully as a fisher of men. This removes the intimidation that Satan would love to throw your way.

The Spiritual Armor

The Purpose of the Spiritual Armor

Eph 6:10 Finally, my brethren, be strong in the Lord, and in the power of his might. **Eph 6:11** Put on the whole armour of God, <u>**that ye may be able to stand against the wiles of the devil.**</u>

Eph 6:12 For we wrestle not against flesh and blood, but against principalities, against powers, against the rulers of the darkness of this world, against spiritual wickedness in high *places*. **Eph 6:13** Wherefore take unto you the whole armour of God, <u>**that ye may be able to withstand in the evil day, and having done all, to stand.**</u>

The purpose of the spiritual armor is not to fight against the lost sinner but to fight for the lost sinner. The spiritual armor is to protect us against whatever Satan will throw at us. Notice below in **Eph. 6:16**, the Armor is designed to "quench all the fiery darts of the wicked." Be careful not to overlook the word "all." That being said, allow me to name a few of the fiery darts of the wicked.

1) **Fear**: **2Tim 1:7** For <u>**God hath not given us the spirit of fear**</u>; but of power, and of love, and of a sound mind.

2) **Doubt**: **Rom 14:23** And he that doubteth is damned if he eat, because *he eateth* not of faith: for <u>**whatsoever *is* not of faith is sin**</u>.

3) **Stress**: **Ps 25:17** The troubles of my heart are enlarged: *O* <u>**bring thou me out of my distresses.**</u>

4) **Hate**: **1John 4:20** <u>**If a man say, I love God, and hateth his brother, he is a liar**</u>: for he that loveth not his brother whom he hath seen, how can he love God whom he hath not seen?

5) **Pride**: **Prov 13:10** <u>**Only by pride cometh contention**</u>: but with the well advised *is* wisdom.

6) **Lust**: **1John 2:16** <u>**For all that *is* in the world, the lust of the flesh, and the lust of the eyes, and the pride of life, is not of the Father, but is of the world.**</u>

7) **Deceit**: Ps 120:2 <u>Deliver my soul, O LORD, from lying lips, *and* from a deceitful tongue.</u>

8) **Distraction: 1Cor 7:35** And this I speak for your own profit; not that I may cast a snare upon you, but for that which is comely, and **that ye may attend upon the Lord without distraction.**

The Parts of the Spiritual Armor

Eph 6:14 Stand therefore, having your loins girt about with **truth**, and having on the breastplate of righteousness;

Eph 6:15 And your feet shod with **the preparation of the gospel of peace**;

> *Notice the word, "preparation." The believer that is constantly prepared and alert to share the gospel with anyone and everyone is considered by Satan to be a very dangerous individual. The fisher of men must always be prepared and set on ready to share the gospel.*

> *The fisher of men must not underestimate the power of the gospel.*

> ***Rom 1:16*** *For* <u>***I am not ashamed of the gospel of Christ: for it is the power of God unto salvation to every one that believeth***</u>; *to the Jew first, and also to the Greek.*

Eph 6:16 Above all, taking the **<u>shield of faith</u>**, wherewith ye shall be able to quench all the fiery darts of the wicked.

Eph 6:17 And take the **<u>helmet of salvation</u>**, and the sword of the Spirit, which is the **<u>word of God:</u>**

Eph 6:18 **<u>Praying</u>** always with all prayer and supplication in the Spirit, and **<u>watching</u>** thereunto with all perseverance and supplication for all saints;

17

Using Some Unusual Tools in Some Unusual Situations

One of the things a "fisher of men" needs to be aware of is that sometimes and in some situations, there are some tools to have with you that can come in very handy. Ordinarily when I go visiting, I have with me a New Testament, Gospel Tracts, a clip board with 8 ½ x 11 sheets of paper with the map of the street and houses that I am visiting at that time and an ink pen.

In unusual situations the soulwinner needs to appeal to God for other tools that God would use to help the visiting to go well. Allow me to illustrate.

Years ago, I was in an area that had a large trailer court in it with over a hundred trailers. I heard by many from many different sources and people from different backgrounds that this particular trailer court was housed with some very dangerous people. Most people feared to go near that particular neighborhood. The police were constantly answering calls from that location.

It also was about this time that I had injured myself playing racquetball on a week-night. I had ruptured my Achilles tendon and had to have emergency surgery. After the surgery and recovery, I was put in a leg brace and was able to maneuver on crutches. At that time, it occurred to me to go visit in that trailer court neighborhood while on crutches. The principle that I had in mind was like the old saying, "you never hit a man with glasses on." Being the brave soul that I was, instead of hiding behind glasses, I was hiding behind the leg brace and crutches and going door to door or trailer to trailer witnessing and passing out tracks. In spite of my cowardice, God gave me some good visits and I was able to get the gospel out to many and tracts were put in every front door of each trailer or in the hand of the people that were home. I even had people come out of their homes and meet me in their driveway and talk with me thinking I needed help. God blessed that time of visitation in spite of me being a coward and used the tools of the leg brace and crutches to reach into a very dangerous neighborhood.

More recently in the time when the covad was going strong, I feared the total shutdown of door-to-door visitation because of the covad. I went to God in prayer and asked God what can I do to keep going on visitation. At this time there also was a shortage of toilet paper and hand sanitizer. I believed that God laid on my heart to do the following.

I went to the store and bought a box of one-gallon zip lock bags, toilet paper as much as I could find, and hand sanitizer. I brought them back to my office at church and put in each one-gallon zip lock bag, one tract, one roll of toilet paper, and one container of hand sanitizer. I made several of these and put four in a plastic bag and filled several bags. With a mask, gloves on hands and these bags as well as my New Testament and Tracts, I proceeded to go door knocking. After knocking on each door of each home I would back up 6 feet from the door and wait for the individual to come to the door. The opening comments changed to something like the following.

Hello, my name is Gerald McDaniel, and I am pastor of "the name of the church" and our church has stocked up on hand sanitizer and toilet paper. It is free. Do you by any chance need any of these supplies?

I was thrilled by the response of the people being visited and how God was using these unusual tools to help me reach the people for Christ. In spite of the covid, people were still getting saved. People reacted very gratefully, and I was even able to give out a lot of toilet paper and hand sanitizer.

Now, for another tool, let us go back to the clip-board. It is not only used for holding paper and writing on it, I had another use in mind as well. If you have ever been to a FFA Fair, I will try to illustrate another use for the clipboard. At the Future Farmers of America fair, it was time for the young people to precent the boar hogs. Several would be out in the arena at the same time with the young people guided each hog. When one hog would try to get rough with another hog, the young people had a wooden board about 4 foot by 4 foot and the young person would slide that board in between the hogs and they would stop trying to fight each other. That is the principle with the clipboard in hand. For example, I was visiting a particular home and talking to a man out in his front yard. As I was talking a dog came out from the back yard and came at me with the intensions of biting me. I quickly placed the clipboard in front of his nose and he stopped advances toward me. I was very thankful and had a new and different appreciation for that particular tool at that time.

Remember, with every obstacle, ask God to help you with some type of special tool to help you get over the obstacle and keep visiting.

18

How to Be Filled with the Holy Spirit

Since the main purpose for being filled with the Holy Spirit is to be a witness for Christ, it is important for the believer to know what the filling of the Holy Spirit is and how to be filled with the Holy Spirit. So, this is the reason for this chapter being attached to this book on being a "Fisher of Men."

One of the conditions for being filled with the Holy Spirit is that the best you can to be totally surrendered to God. Note the following passage:

***Romans 12:**1 I beseech you therefore, brethren, by the mercies of God, that ye present your bodies a living sacrifice, holy, acceptable unto God, *which is* your reasonable service. **2** And be not conformed to this world: but be ye transformed by the renewing of your mind, **that ye may prove what *is* that good, and acceptable, and perfect, will of God.**

The cultivation of the believer is not only a must for knowing God's will, it is a must for being filled with the Holy Spirit and becoming a successful "Fisher of Men." Without turning your life totally over to God you will not be able to be filled with the Holy Spirit and be a fisher of men.

Witnessing is one of five grooming tools that every believer has when applied to their lives faithfully will bring spiritual growth, help groom, and polish the believer and bring assurance of God's will to them. They are as follows:

1) Attending Church:

   Hebrews 10:25 <u>Not forsaking the assembling of ourselves together,</u> as the manner of some *is*; but exhorting *one another*: and so much the more, as ye see the day approaching.

2) Praying:

   1 Thessalonians 5:17 <u>Pray</u> without ceasing.

3) Giving:

   Luke 6:38 <u>Give,</u> and it shall be given unto you; good measure, pressed down, and shaken together, and running over, shall men give into your bosom. For with the same measure that ye mete withal it shall be measured to you again.

4) Studying the Bible:

> **2 Timothy 2:15** <u>Study </u>to shew thyself approved unto God, a workman that needeth not to be ashamed, rightly dividing the word of truth.

5) Witnessing.

> **Matthew 28:19-20** Go ye therefore, and <u>teach all nations</u>, baptizing them in the name of the Father, and of the Son, and of the Holy Ghost: **20** Teaching them to observe all things whatsoever I have commanded you: and, lo, I am with you alway, *even* unto the end of the world. Amen.

These are not the type of commandments that you obey one time and are done such as getting baptized. These commands are to be maintained in the believer's life. Any believer can do these simple tasks and are commanded by God to maintain these commandments. This will bring about spiritual growth.

See the following verses in the New Testament using the term "filled with the Holy Spirit."

Luke 1:15 For he shall be great in the sight of the Lord, and shall drink neither wine nor strong drink; and he shall <u>be filled with the Holy Ghost</u>, even from his mother's womb.

Luke 1:41 And it came to pass, that, when Elisabeth heard the salutation of Mary, the babe leaped in her womb; and Elisabeth was <u>filled with the Holy Ghost</u>:

Acts 4:8 Then Peter, <u>filled with the Holy Ghost</u>, said unto them, Ye rulers of the people, and elders of Israel,

Acts 9:17 And Ananias went his way, and entered into the house; and putting his hands on him said, Brother Saul, the Lord, *even* Jesus, that appeared unto thee in the way as thou camest, hath sent me, that thou mightest receive thy sight, and be <u>filled with the Holy Ghost</u>.

Acts 13:9 Then Saul, (who also *is called* Paul,) <u>filled with the Holy Ghost</u>, set his eyes on him,

Acts 13:52 And the disciples were <u>filled with joy, and with the Holy Ghost</u>.

Ephesians 3:19 And to know the love of Christ, which passeth knowledge, that ye might be <u>filled with all the fulness of God.</u>

It must be noted that there are different phrases that God uses that refer to the same event of being filled with the Holy Ghost. See the following examples:

1) Endued with power from on high.

   Luke 24:49 And, behold, I send the promise of my Father upon you: but tarry ye in the city of

Jerusalem, until **ye be endued with power from on high**.

2)   The Spirit of God coming upon you or on you.

Acts 8:15 Who, when they were come down, prayed for them, that **they might receive the Holy Ghost**: **16** (For as yet **he was fallen upon none of them**: only they were baptized in the name of the Lord Jesus.) **17** Then laid they *their* hands on them, and **they received the Holy Ghost**.

Mat. 12:18 Behold my servant, whom I have chosen; my beloved, in whom my soul is well pleased: **I will put my spirit upon him**, and he shall shew judgment to the Gentiles.

Luke 1:35 And the angel answered and said unto her**, the Holy Ghost shall come upon thee**, and the power of the Highest shall overshadow thee: therefore also that holy thing which shall be born of thee shall be called the Son of God.

Luke 2:25 And, behold, there was a man in Jerusalem, whose name was Simeon; and the same man was just and devout, waiting for the consolation of Israel: and **the Holy Ghost was upon him.**

Luke 24:49 And, behold**, I send the promise of my Father upon you**: but tarry ye in the city of Jerusalem, until ye be endued with power from on high.

Acts 10:44 While Peter yet spake these words, **the Holy Ghost fell on all them** which heard the word.

Acts 11:15 And as I began to speak, **the Holy Ghost fell on them** as on us in the beginning.

3) Being baptized with the Holy Ghost.

Matthew 3:11 I indeed baptize you with water unto repentance: but he that cometh after me is mightier than I, whose shoes I am not worthy to bear: he shall **baptize you with the Holy Ghost**, and *with* fire:

Mark 1:8 I indeed have baptized you with water: but **he shall baptize you with the Holy Ghost**.

Luke 3:16 John answered, saying unto *them* all, I indeed baptize you with water; but one mightier than I cometh, the latchet of whose shoes I am not worthy to unloose: **he shall baptize you with the Holy Ghost** and with fire:

John 1:33 And I knew him not: but he that sent me to baptize with water, the same said unto me,

Upon whom thou shalt see the Spirit descending, and remaining on him, the same is **he which baptizeth with the Holy Ghost.**

Acts 1:5 For John truly baptized with water; but ye shall be **baptized with the Holy Ghost** not many days hence.

This passage makes it clear that the individuals were already saved and the "not many days hence" is a reference to being filled with the Holy Ghost later on in their lives.

Though the above scripture references refer to being filled with the Holy Ghost, the reader must be aware that this must not be confused with the act of God that takes place when the person upon salvation is indwelt with the Holy Spirit and baptized into the body of Christ by the Holy Ghost. That spiritual baptism occurs automatically upon trusting Christ as Savior. See the following passages for this baptism.

1 Corinthians 12:13 **For by one Spirit are we all baptized into one body**, whether *we be* Jews or Gentiles, whether *we be* bond or free; and have been all made to drink into one Spirit.

Galatians 3:27 For **as many of you as have been baptized into Christ have put on Christ**.

John 7:37–39 In the last day, that great day of the feast, Jesus stood and cried, saying, If any man thirst, let him come unto me, and drink. **38** He that believeth on me, as the scripture hath said, out of his belly shall flow rivers of living water. **39** (<u>**But this spake he of the Spirit, which they that believe on him should receive**</u>: for the Holy Ghost was not yet given; because that Jesus was not yet glorified.)

Ephesians 1:13 In whom ye also trusted, after that ye heard the word of truth, the gospel of your salvation: in whom also <u>**after that ye believed, ye were sealed with that holy Spirit of promise,**</u>

Ephesians 4:30 And grieve not <u>**the holy Spirit of God, whereby ye are sealed**</u> unto the day of redemption.

Galatians 3:2 This only would I learn of you, <u>**Received ye the Spirit**</u> by the works of the law, or <u>**by the hearing of faith**</u>?

Galatians 3:14 That the blessing of Abraham might come on the Gentiles through Jesus Christ; that <u>**we might receive the promise of the Spirit through faith.**</u>

How to be Filled with the Holy Spirit

Ephesians 5:18 And be not drunk with wine, wherein is excess; but <u>be **filled (#4137)** with the Spirit</u>;

Notice the word study sentence on "filled."

"filled" #4137 (90x)(fulfil-51; fill-19; be full-7; complete-2; end-2; accomplish; expired; supply; perfect; preached; misc-4)

The following are simple steps to guide the believer into being filled with the Holy Spirit.

1) The individual must be saved.

    The number one rule is in order to be filled with the Holy Spirit you must first be born of the Holy Spirit. Please read Chapter 1 and make sure that you are born again.

2) Be humbled and surrendered

    Romans 12:1 1 I beseech you therefore, brethren, by the mercies of God, that ye present your bodies a living sacrifice, holy, acceptable unto God, *which is* your reasonable service. **2** And be not conformed to this world: but be ye transformed by the renewing of your mind, that ye may prove what *is* that good, and acceptable, and perfect, will of God.

    Note: You cannot have a humble life without a surrendered life. These two go hand in hand. You cannot have a surrendered life and be living in pride.

3) Saturate yourself with the Scriptures

> ***Colossians 3:16*** <u>Let the word of Christ dwell in you richly</u> in all wisdom; teaching and admonishing one another in psalms and hymns and spiritual songs, singing with grace in your hearts to the Lord.

4) Develop a strong affection for loving right and hating wrong

> ***Hebrews 1:9*** Thou hast loved righteousness, and hated iniquity; therefore God, *even* thy God, hath anointed thee with the oil of gladness above thy fellows.

> *Note: The more you love what is right and hate what is wrong the more you will be able to be filled with the Holy Spirit.*

5) Having a strong desire to be controlled by God and filled with the Holy Spirit.

> ***Matthew 5:6*** Blessed *are* they which do <u>hunger and thirst after righteousness: for they shall be filled</u>.

> ***Luke 6:21*** Blessed *are ye* that <u>hunger now: for ye shall be filled</u>. Blessed *are ye* that weep now: for ye shall laugh.

Luke 22:42 Saying, Father, if thou be willing, remove this cup from me: nevertheless <u>not my will, but thine, be done.</u>

6) Ask God to fill you with the Holy Ghost.

Luke 11:13 If ye then, being evil, know how to give good gifts unto your children: <u>how much more shall *your* heavenly Father give the Holy Spirit to them that ask him?</u>

James 4:2 Ye lust, and have not: ye kill, and desire to have, and cannot obtain: ye fight and war, yet **ye have not, because ye ask not**.

Evidence of being filled with the Holy Spirit

Ephesians 5:18 And be not drunk with wine, wherein is excess; but <u>be filled with the Spirit</u>; **19** Speaking to yourselves in psalms and hymns and spiritual songs, singing and making melody in your heart to the Lord; **20** Giving thanks always for all things unto God and the Father in the name of our Lord Jesus Christ; **21** Submitting yourselves one to another in the fear of God.

1) **A song in your heart**
Verse **19** Speaking to yourselves in psalms and hymns and spiritual songs, singing and making melody in your heart to the Lord;

The person that listens to worldly music and is filled with worldly music instead of godly Christian music is not filled with the Holy Spirit.

2) **Thanksgiving**
Verse **20** Giving thanks always for all things unto God and the Father in the name of our Lord Jesus Christ;

The person that is griping and complaining about things in their life instead of being thankful is not filled with the Holy Spirit.

3) **Submission to authority**
Verse **21** Submitting yourselves one to another in the fear of God.

The person that is rebellious against authority instead of submitting to authority is not filled with the Holy Spirit.

4) **Displaying the Fruit of the Spirit in the Believer's Character**
Galatians 5:22 But the fruit of the Spirit is **love, joy, peace, longsuffering, gentleness, goodness, faith, 23 Meekness, temperance**: against such there is no law.

The Purpose of being filled with the Holy Spirit

Please understand that an individual is not filled with the Holy Spirit just for the sake of being filled with the Holy Spirit. The purpose of being filled with the Holy Spirit is to perform a particular task that God has for them to do. The believer that stays seated on the pew and does nothing for God will know nothing of being filled with the Holy Ghost. **Typically, the main reason for the filling of the Holy Spirit is to enable the believer to witness and testify to the lost with boldness and authority.**

Acts 4:31 And when they had prayed, the place was shaken where they were assembled together; and **they were all filled with the Holy Ghost, and they spake the word of God with boldness.**

The believer that has no interest in witnessing and spreading the gospel also knows nothing about being filled with the Holy Spirit.

Notice these other passages.

Acts 1:8 But **ye shall receive power, after that the Holy Ghost is come upon you: and ye shall be witnesses** unto me both in Jerusalem, and in all Judaea, and in Samaria, and unto the uttermost part of the earth.

Luke 4:18 The Spirit of the Lord is upon me, because he hath anointed me to preach the gospel to the poor;

he hath sent me to heal the brokenhearted, to preach deliverance to the captives, and recovering of sight to the blind, to set at liberty them that are bruised,

The person that is about to teach a Sunday School class needs to be filled with the Holy Spirit. The person that is about to preach needs to be filled with the Holy Spirit. A person that is about to go soul winning needs to be filled with the Holy Spirit. However, the believer who is doing nothing will know nothing of being filled with the Holy Spirit.

19

Humble Pie

One of the things you are going to have to eat to be a "fisher of men" is a lot of humble pie. You must be prepared to be cursed at for no reason or to be chewed out for simply walking down someone's driveway. Some people will get quite hostile with you, but you must not retaliate in anyway. You must understand witnessing is a very important work for God, but it also puts the soulwinning believer on the front lines of the battlefield. You are popular in heaven for giving out the gospel but on earth, not so much. You will find out very soon where Satan's resistance is. That is why this author mentioned previously in this book about the spiritual armor and being filled with the Holy Spirit and using your Bible which is the sword of the Lord. You will learn new meaning to the expression. "Turning the other cheek."

It is thrilling to lead someone to Christ, but the believer must be aware that this does not take place all the time nor every time you go out. Allow me to illustrate from my own personal experience. Presently during the writing of this book by the grace of God I am seeing one person saved per everyone hundred doors that I knock on. This streak so far has lasted for four years. Before this streak started, I was in some very long steaks of seeing no one saved. You will go through long streaks of having no one saved but you must stay with it.

Remember because you are rare as a "fisher of men" you are not going to be appreciated by most believers. They will not realize the sacrifice that you make to spread the gospel or the spiritual battle that you are in. If you are getting into soulwinning to be popular in church, you are in it for the wrong reason. Instead of a congratulations coming from some believers you might get a response like the following. "How do you know they really got saved?" The simple answer to that is you take their word for it just like you take anyone's word for it.

Typically, the one that will appreciate you the most down here on earth is another "fisher of men." If I have a chance to lead someone to Christ, sometimes I will call another soulwinner that I know and share and rejoice with him or her over the soul that was saved.

You must not allow yourself to get some kind of vain persecution complex are seek for pity from anyone.

If you will notice the passages below and meditate on them regularly you will be reminded that God appreciates what you are doing, and He is the one that counts. Remember what the unbelieving world did to Jesus. However, the unbelieving world is the harvest field that all believers are working in and every soul is precious.

(Mic 6:8) He hath shewed thee, O man, **what *is* good; and what doth the LORD require of thee, but to do justly, and to love mercy, and to walk humbly with thy God?**

(Jas 4:6) But he giveth more grace. Wherefore he saith, **God resisteth the proud, but giveth grace unto the humble.**

(Jas 4:10) Humble yourselves in the sight of the Lord, and he shall lift you up.

(1Pet 5:6) Humble yourselves therefore under the mighty hand of God, that he may exalt you in due time:

So, simply put, if you are having trouble with pride in your life, you have not been soulwinning enough. To close this book out, I would like to share with the reader a poem I have written.

I Am Afraid

If we are not careful, we will have children and adults
Instead of trusting the requirement for
heaven they will trust in the results.
They will trust in the prayer that was prayed
instead of the price that was paid.
They will trust in their call instead
of the One who paid it all.
They will trust in the one that shared
instead of the Christ who cared.
They will trust in a time of sorrow instead
of the One who holds tomorrow.
They will trust in turning from sin instead
of the One that paid for their sin.
They will trust in the changes they made
instead of Jesus and the price He paid.
Many, who trust the cross of Christ
instead of the Christ of the cross,
Will receive false security not realizing
that they are still lost.
If the one witnessing is not careful
and too anxious to see results
Will have the sinner trust in something besides
Jesus and join along with the cults.
Salvation is not a process going through step A, B, or C
It is instant in Jesus because He died for us to set us free.
Whether you walk a church isle or bend a knee
Salvation is in Christ and absolutely free.

Salvation is not a process of our emotions
of sorrow or fear or love.
Salvation is instant in Christ who
came down from heaven above.
I am afraid, though well meaning, preachers
and teachers sharing the word
Leave the wrong impression to the sinner
and the way of salvation is blurred.
It is true we have sinned, and it is Hell we deserve
And our lives were ruined, and it
was Satan who we served.
But after trusting Christ we must reassure the lost
sinner that the way to heaven has been paved
The Bible says, "believe on the Lord Jesus
Christ and thou shalt be saved."

Remember dear soulwinner and fisher of men, remind the
lost sinner that it is what Jesus did, not what they do, that
they should depend on to get them to heaven.

Printed in the United States
by Baker & Taylor Publisher Services